INFERNO

INFERNO

DANTE ALIGHIERI

This edition published in 2019 by Arcturus Publishing Limited
26/27 Bickels Yard, 151–153 Bermondsey Street,
London SE1 3HA

Cover design: Peter Ridley
Cover illustration: Peter Gray
Design: Catherine Wood

AD006527UK

Printed in the UK

Contents

Cantos

Introduction

Dante Alighieri (1265–1321) was born into a noble Florentine family in a city torn apart by rival clans. While feudal aristocracy backed imperial authority (Ghibellines), the Alighieri family supported the pope (Guelphs). Their party eventually splintered into hostile White and Black factions. Offended by Pope Boniface VIII's interference in secular affairs, Dante, too, became embroiled in this sectarianism and joined the White Guelphs. He was banished following the Black Guelph victory of 1302. Although he enjoyed the patronage of powerful northern Italian princes, his future political allegiances were misguided. He died in exile in Ravenna in 1321.

The Divine Comedy, the first book to be written in the Italian *vulgare* instead of Latin, was begun in 1308 and contains three *cantiche* – *Inferno* (Hell), *Purgatorio* (Purgatory) and *Paradiso* (Paradise) – written in *terza rima*, a verse scheme of three-line stanzas with interlocking rhyme patterns (aba, bcb, cdc and so on). Dante's influences included the classics, the neo-Platonists, Aristotle, natural philosophy and theology. The *Inferno's* opening canto is a microcosm of the entire work and its topography prefigures the three realms of the soul's afterlife: the dark wood (Hell), the barren slope (Mount Purgatory) and the blissful mountain (Paradise).

The epic poem juxtaposes human privation, injustice and imperfection with divine freedom, justice and perfection. Dante's allegorical theme of God's gradual revelation to an unsuspecting, unprepared pilgrim beautifully illustrates the concept of the rational human soul choosing salvation of its own free will. The use of real-life characters, autobiographical detail, personal failures and triumphs, sophisticated eschatological discourse and the denunciation of contemporary politics renders the poem unique.

The technique of having two Dante characters, the Poet and the Pilgrim, allows the narrative to reach out to the universal reader whilst operating on a personal level. During his spiritual journey, the pilgrim participates in the sin of every sinner, the penance of every repentant soul and the bliss of the blessed – he is Everyman.

Hell *(Inferno)*
At the age of thirty-five Dante is lost in a dark forest, having missed the "straightforward way". The way to salvation is symbolised by the sun behind the mountain but it is barred by a Leopard, a Lion and a She-Wolf. The beasts represent different sins. After Dante's love, Beatrice, intercedes on his behalf he is joined by the poet Virgil, who becomes his guide through the underworld. They cross the Acheron, on Charon's ferry, and reach the Gate of Hell. From there they descend through the nine Circles of Hell, each circle representing a different sin. The punishments are chillingly appropriate. They finally reach the lake of ice where the three-headed Lucifer resides. Each head

is chewing a sinner (Judas, Brutus and Cassius). The pair escape by climbing down Lucifer's furry legs. After passing through the centre of the Earth, they emerge to "rebehold the stars".

❧CANTO I

In the middle of his life, Dante has left the "straightforward pathway" and is lost in a dark forest. He tries to regain the path by climbing a mountain but his way is barred by a Leopard, a Lion and a She-Wolf. Each creature represents a different sin. Virgil appears and offers to show him another way, one that leads through Hell and Purgatory. After that, a "more worthy" guide (Beatrice) will lead him to Paradise: Virgil, as a Pagan, is not allowed to go there. Dante gladly adopts Virgil as his leader.

Midway upon the journey of our life
  I found myself within a forest dark,
  For the straightforward pathway had been lost.

Ah me! how hard a thing it is to say
  What was this forest savage, rough, and stern,
  Which in the very thought renews the fear.

So bitter is it, death is little more;
  But of the good to treat, which there I found,
  Speak will I of the other things I saw there.

I cannot well repeat how there I entered,
  So full was I of slumber at the moment
  In which I had abandoned the true way.

But after I had reached a mountain's foot,
  At that point where the valley terminated,
  Which had with consternation pierced my heart,

Upward I looked, and I beheld its shoulders,
  Vested already with that planet's rays
  Which leadeth others right by every road.

Then was the fear a little quieted
  That in my heart's lake had endured throughout
  The night, which I had passed so piteously.

And even as he, who, with distressful breath,
  Forth issued from the sea upon the shore,
  Turns to the water perilous and gazes;

So did my soul, that still was fleeing onward,
  Turn itself back to re-behold the pass
  Which never yet a living person left.

After my weary body I had rested,
  The way resumed I on the desert slope,
  So that the firm foot ever was the lower.

And lo! Almost where the ascent began,
  A panther light and swift exceedingly,
  Which with a spotted skin was covered o'er!

And never moved she from before my face,
  Nay, rather did impede so much my way,
  That many times I to return had turned.

The time was the beginning of the morning,
  And up the sun was mounting with those stars
  That with him were, what time the Love Divine

At first in motion set those beauteous things;
  So were to me occasion of good hope,
  The variegated skin of that wild beast,

The hour of time, and the delicious season;
  But not so much, that did not give me fear
  A lion's aspect which appeared to me.

He seemed as if against me he were coming
  With head uplifted, and with ravenous hunger,
  So that it seemed the air was afraid of him;

And a she-wolf, that with all hungerings
   Seemed to be laden in her meagreness,
   And many folk has caused to live forlorn!

She brought upon me so much heaviness,
   With the affright that from her aspect came,
   That I the hope relinquished of the height.

And as he is who willingly acquires,
   And the time comes that causes him to lose,
   Who weeps in all his thoughts and is despondent,

E'en such made me that beast withouten peace,
   Which, coming on against me by degrees
   Thrust me back thither where the sun is silent.

While I was rushing downward to the lowland,
   Before mine eyes did one present himself,
   Who seemed from long-continued silence hoarse.

When I beheld him in the desert vast,
   "Have pity on me," unto him I cried,
   "Whiche'er thou art, or shade or real man!"

He answered me: "Not man; man once I was,
   And both my parents were of Lombardy,
   And Mantuans by country both of them.

Sub Julio was I born, though it was late,
   And lived at Rome under the good Augustus,
   During the time of false and lying gods.

A poet was I, and I sang that just
   Son of Anchises, who came forth from Troy,
   After that Ilion the superb was burned.

But thou, why goest thou back to such annoyance?
   Why climb'st thou not the Mount Delectable,
   Which is the source and cause of every joy?"

"Now, art thou that Virgilius and that fountain
  Which spreads abroad so wide a river of speech?"
  I made response to him with bashful forehead.

"O, of the other poets honour and light,
  Avail me the long study and great love
  That have impelled me to explore thy volume!

Thou art my master, and my author thou,
  Thou art alone the one from whom I took
  The beautiful style that has done honour to me.

Behold the beast, for which I have turned back;
  Do thou protect me from her, famous Sage,
  For she doth make my veins and pulses tremble."

"Thee it behoves to take another road,"
  Responded he, when he beheld me weeping,
  "If from this savage place thou wouldst escape;

Because this beast, at which thou criest out,
  Suffers not any one to pass her way,
  But so doth harass him, that she destroys him;

And has a nature so malign and ruthless,
  That never doth she glut her greedy will,
  And after food is hungrier than before.

Many the animals with whom she weds,
  And more they shall be still, until the Greyhound
  Comes, who shall make her perish in her pain.

He shall not feed on either earth or pelf,
  But upon wisdom, and on love and virtue;
  'Twixt Feltro and Feltro shall his nation be;

Of that low Italy shall he be the saviour,
  On whose account the maid Camilla died,
  Euryalus, Turnus, Nisus, of their wounds;

Through every city shall he hunt her down,
  Until he shall have driven her back to Hell,
  There from whence envy first did let her loose.

Therefore I think and judge it for thy best
  Thou follow me, and I will be thy guide,
  And lead thee hence through the eternal place,

Where thou shalt hear the desperate lamentations,
  Shalt see the ancient spirits disconsolate,
  Who cry out each one for the second death;

And thou shalt see those who contented are
  Within the fire, because they hope to come,
  Whene'er it may be, to the blessed people;

To whom, then, if thou wishest to ascend,
  A soul shall be for that than I more worthy;
  With her at my departure I will leave thee;

Because that Emperor, who reigns above,
  In that I was rebellious to his law,
  Wills that through me none come into his city.

He governs everywhere, and there he reigns;
  There is his city and his lofty throne;
  O happy he whom thereto he elects!"

And I to him: "Poet, I thee entreat,
  By that same God whom thou didst never know,
  So that I may escape this woe and worse,

Thou wouldst conduct me there where thou hast said,
  That I may see the portal of Saint Peter,
  And those thou makest so disconsolate."

Then he moved on, and I behind him followed.

☙CANTO II

The end of the day has come and Dante is having doubts.
He does not feel worthy enough to undertake his journey.
Virgil accuses him of cowardice and tells of how the Virgin
Mary turned to Saint Lucia, who in turn asked for Beatrice,
Dante's love, to go down into Limbo, where Virgil resides.
There Beatrice, with "voice angelical", asked Virgil to assist
Dante, whose way was impeded. At this, Dante is heartened,
and declares to Virgil that "one sole will is in us both".

Day was departing, and the embrowned air
  Released the animals that are on Earth
  From their fatigues; and I the only one

Made myself ready to sustain the war,
  Both of the way and likewise of the woe,
  Which memory that errs not shall retrace.

O Muses, O high genius, now assist me!
  O memory, that didst write down what I saw,
  Here thy nobility shall be manifest!

And I began: "Poet, who guidest me,
  Regard my manhood, if it be sufficient,
  Ere to the arduous pass thou dost confide me.

Thou sayest, that of Silvius the parent,
  While yet corruptible, unto the world
  Immortal went, and was there bodily.

But if the adversary of all evil
  Was courteous, thinking of the high effect
  That issue would from him, and who, and what,

To men of intellect unmeet it seems not;
  For he was of great Rome, and of her empire
  In the empyreal heaven as father chosen;

The which and what, wishing to speak the truth,
  Were stablished as the holy place, wherein
  Sits the successor of the greatest Peter.

Upon this journey, whence thou givest him vaunt,
  Things did he hear, which the occasion were
  Both of his victory and the papal mantle.

Thither went afterwards the Chosen Vessel,
  To bring back comfort thence unto that Faith,
  Which of salvation's way is the beginning.

But I, why thither come, or who concedes it?
  I not Aeneas am, I am not Paul,
  Nor I, nor others, think me worthy of it.

Therefore, if I resign myself to come,
  I fear the coming may be ill-advised;
  Thou'rt wise, and knowest better than I speak."

And as he is, who unwills what he willed,
  And by new thoughts doth his intention change,
  So that from his design he quite withdraws,

Such I became, upon that dark hillside,
  Because, in thinking, I consumed the emprise,
  Which was so very prompt in the beginning.

"If I have well thy language understood,"
  Replied that shade of the Magnanimous,
  "Thy soul attainted is with cowardice,

Which many times a man encumbers so,
  It turns him back from honoured enterprise,
  As false sight doth a beast, when he is shy.

That thou mayst free thee from this apprehension,
  I'll tell thee why I came, and what I heard
  At the first moment when I grieved for thee.

Among those was I who are in suspense,
  And a fair, saintly Lady called to me
  In such wise, I besought her to command me.

Her eyes were shining brighter than the Star;
  And she began to say, gentle and low,
  With voice angelical, in her own language:

'O spirit courteous of Mantua,
  Of whom the fame still in the world endures,
  And shall endure, long-lasting as the world;

A friend of mine, and not the friend of fortune,
  Upon the desert slope is so impeded
  Upon his way, that he has turned through terror,

And may, I fear, already be so lost,
  That I too late have risen to his succour,
  From that which I have heard of him in Heaven.

Bestir thee now, and with thy speech ornate,
  And with what needful is for his release,
  Assist him so, that I may be consoled.

Beatrice am I, who do bid thee go;
  I come from there, where I would fain return;
  Love moved me, which compelleth me to speak.

When I shall be in presence of my Lord,
  Full often will I praise thee unto him.'
  Then paused she, and thereafter I began:

'O Lady of virtue, thou alone through whom
  The human race exceedeth all contained
  Within the heaven that has the lesser circles,

So grateful unto me is thy commandment,
  To obey, if 'twere already done, were late;
  No farther need'st thou ope to me thy wish.

But the cause tell me why thou dost not shun
  The here descending down into this centre,
  From the vast place thou burnest to return to.'

'Since thou wouldst fain so inwardly discern,
  Briefly will I relate,' she answered me,
  'Why I am not afraid to enter here.

Of those things only should one be afraid
  Which have the power of doing others harm;
  Of the rest, no; because they are not fearful.

God in his mercy such created me
  That misery of yours attains me not,
  Nor any flame assails me of this burning.

A gentle Lady is in Heaven, who grieves
  At this impediment, to which I send thee,
  So that stern judgment there above is broken.

In her entreaty she besought Lucia,
  And said, "Thy faithful one now stands in need
  Of thee, and unto thee I recommend him."

Lucia, foe of all that cruel is,
  Hastened away, and came unto the place
  Where I was sitting with the ancient Rachel.

"Beatrice" said she, "the true praise of God,
  Why succourest thou not him, who loved thee so,
  For thee he issued from the vulgar herd?

Dost thou not hear the pity of his plaint?
  Dost thou not see the death that combats him
  Beside that flood, where ocean has no vaunt?"

Never were persons in the world so swift
  To work their weal and to escape their woe,
  As I, after such words as these were uttered,

Came hither downward from my blessed seat,
  Confiding in thy dignified discourse,
  Which honours thee, and those who've listened to it.'

After she thus had spoken unto me,
  Weeping, her shining eyes she turned away;
  Whereby she made me swifter in my coming;

And unto thee I came, as she desired;
  I have delivered thee from that wild beast,
  Which barred the beautiful mountain's short ascent.

What is it, then? Why, why dost thou delay?
  Why is such baseness bedded in thy heart?
  Daring and hardihood why hast thou not,

Seeing that three such Ladies benedight
  Are caring for thee in the court of Heaven,
  And so much good my speech doth promise thee?"

Even as the flowerets, by nocturnal chill,
  Bowed down and closed, when the sun whitens them,
  Uplift themselves all open on their stems;

Such I became with my exhausted strength,
  And such good courage to my heart there coursed,
  That I began, like an intrepid person:

"O she compassionate, who succoured me,
  And courteous thou, who hast obeyed so soon
  The words of truth which she addressed to thee!

Thou hast my heart so with desire disposed
  To the adventure, with these words of thine,
  That to my first intent I have returned.

Now go, for one sole will is in us both,
  Thou Leader, and thou Lord, and Master thou."
  Thus said I to him; and when he had moved,

I entered on the deep and savage way.

⚘CANTO III

As Dante and Virgil enter Hell's ante-chamber, they see words
inscribed above its gate and hear the cries of the Indecisive, the
first group of damned souls. These moral "cowards", rejected
by Heaven yet ignored by Hell, have to chase a banner whilst
being plagued by hornets and flies. Charon the Boatman
refuses to carry Dante, a living soul, across the river Acheron
on Hell's outer boundary, but Virgil declares that Heaven wills
it. A fierce wind picks up and Dante swoons.

"Through me the way is to the city dolent;
  Through me the way is to eternal dole;
  Through me the way among the people lost.

Justice incited my sublime Creator;
  Created me divine Omnipotence,
  The highest Wisdom and the primal Love.

Before me there were no created things,
  Only eterne, and I eternal last.
  All hope abandon, ye who enter in!"

These words in sombre colour I beheld
  Written upon the summit of a gate;
  Whence I: "Their sense is, Master, hard to me!"

And he to me, as one experienced:
  "Here all suspicion needs must be abandoned,
  All cowardice must needs be here extinct.

We to the place have come, where I have told thee
  Thou shalt behold the people dolorous
  Who have foregone the good of intellect."

And after he had laid his hand on mine
  With joyful mien, whence I was comforted,
  He led me in among the secret things.

There sighs, complaints, and ululations loud
  Resounded through the air without a star,
  Whence I, at the beginning, wept thereat.

Languages diverse, horrible dialects,
  Accents of anger, words of agony,
  And voices high and hoarse, with sound of hands,

Made up a tumult that goes whirling on
  For ever in that air for ever black,
  Even as the sand doth, when the whirlwind breathes.

And I, who had my head with horror bound,
  Said: "Master, what is this which now I hear?
  What folk is this, which seems by pain so vanquished?"

And he to me: "This miserable mode
  Maintain the melancholy souls of those
  Who lived withouten infamy or praise.

Commingled are they with that caitiff choir
  Of Angels, who have not rebellious been,
  Nor faithful were to God, but were for self.

The heavens expelled them, not to be less fair;
  Nor them the nethermore abyss receives,
  For glory none the damned would have from them."

And I: "O Master, what so grievous is
  To these, that maketh them lament so sore?"
  He answered: "I will tell thee very briefly.

These have no longer any hope of death;
  And this blind life of theirs is so debased,
  They envious are of every other fate.

No fame of them the world permits to be;
  Misericord and Justice both disdain them.
  Let us not speak of them, but look, and pass."

And I, who looked again, beheld a banner,
  Which, whirling round, ran on so rapidly,
  That of all pause it seemed to me indignant;

And after it there came so long a train
  Of people, that I ne'er would have believed
  That ever Death so many had undone.

When some among them I had recognised,
  I looked, and I beheld the shade of him
  Who made through cowardice the great refusal.

Forthwith I comprehended, and was certain,
  That this the sect was of the caitiff wretches
  Hateful to God and to his enemies.

These miscreants, who never were alive,
  Were naked, and were stung exceedingly
  By gadflies and by hornets that were there.

These did their faces irrigate with blood,
  Which, with their tears commingled, at their feet
  By the disgusting worms was gathered up.

And when to gazing farther I betook me,
  People I saw on a great river's bank;
  Whence said I: "Master, now vouchsafe to me,

That I may know who these are, and what law
  Makes them appear so ready to pass over,
  As I discern athwart the dusky light."

And he to me: "These things shall all be known
  To thee, as soon as we our footsteps stay
  Upon the dismal shore of Acheron."

Then with mine eyes ashamed and downward cast,
  Fearing my words might irksome be to him,
  From speech refrained I till we reached the river.

And lo! Towards us coming in a boat
  An old man, hoary with the hair of eld,
  Crying: "Woe unto you, ye souls depraved!

Hope nevermore to look upon the heavens;
  I come to lead you to the other shore,
  To the eternal shades in heat and frost.

And thou, that yonder standest, living soul,
  Withdraw thee from these people, who are dead!"
  But when he saw that I did not withdraw,

He said: "By other ways, by other ports
  Thou to the shore shalt come, not here, for passage;
  A lighter vessel needs must carry thee."

And unto him the Guide: "Vex thee not, Charon;
  It is so willed there where is power to do
  That which is willed; and farther question not."

Thereat were quieted the fleecy cheeks
  Of him the ferryman of the livid fen,
  Who round about his eyes had wheels of flame.

But all those souls who weary were and naked
  Their colour changed and gnashed their teeth together,
  As soon as they had heard those cruel words.

God they blasphemed and their progenitors,
  The human race, the place, the time, the seed
  Of their engendering and of their birth!

Thereafter all together they drew back,
  Bitterly weeping, to the accursed shore,
  Which waiteth every man who fears not God.

Charon the demon, with the eyes of glede,
  Beckoning to them, collects them all together,
  Beats with his oar whoever lags behind.

As in the autumn-time the leaves fall off,
  First one and then another, till the branch
  Unto the earth surrenders all its spoils;

In similar wise the evil seed of Adam
  Throw themselves from that margin one by one,
  At signals, as a bird unto its lure.

So they depart across the dusky wave,
  And ere upon the other side they land,
  Again on this side a new troop assembles.

"My son," the courteous Master said to me,
  "All those who perish in the wrath of God
  Here meet together out of every land;

And ready are they to pass o'er the river,
  Because celestial Justice spurs them on,
  So that their fear is turned into desire.

This way there never passes a good soul;
  And hence if Charon doth complain of thee,
  Well mayst thou know now what his speech imports."

This being finished, all the dusk champaign
  Trembled so violently, that of that terror
  The recollection bathes me still with sweat.

The land of tears gave forth a blast of wind,
  And fulminated a vermilion light,
  Which overmastered in me every sense,

And as a man whom sleep hath seized I fell.

CANTO IV

Virgil shows Dante the mournful shadows of virtuous non-Christians like himself who haunt Limbo, Hell's First Circle, and suffer the spiritual torment of forever seeking God in vain. Virgil speaks about Christ's descent into Hell and his salvation of several Old Testament patriarchs. A glowing light reveals four other great pagan figures – Homer, Horace, Ovid and Lucan. The pilgrim perceives a splendid castle of light in the distance, where the most renowned non-Christian philosophers, poets and warriors dwell.

Broke the deep lethargy within my head
  A heavy thunder, so that I upstarted,
  Like to a person who by force is wakened;

And round about I moved my rested eyes,
  Uprisen erect, and steadfastly I gazed,
  To recognise the place wherein I was.

True is it, that upon the verge I found me
  Of the abysmal valley dolorous,
  That gathers thunder of infinite ululations.

Obscure, profound it was, and nebulous,
  So that by fixing on its depths my sight
  Nothing whatever I discerned therein.

"Let us descend now into the blind world,"
  Began the Poet, pallid utterly;
  "I will be first, and thou shalt second be."

And I, who of his colour was aware,
  Said: "How shall I come, if thou art afraid,
  Who'rt wont to be a comfort to my fears?"

And he to me: "The anguish of the people
  Who are below here in my face depicts
  That pity which for terror thou hast taken.

Let us go on, for the long way impels us."
  Thus he went in, and thus he made me enter
  The foremost circle that surrounds the abyss.

There, as it seemed to me from listening,
  Were lamentations none, but only sighs,
  That tremble made the everlasting air.

And this arose from sorrow without torment,
  Which the crowds had, that many were and great,
  Of infants and of women and of men.

To me the Master good: "Thou dost not ask
  What spirits these, which thou beholdest, are?
  Now will I have thee know, ere thou go farther,

That they sinned not; and if they merit had,
  'Tis not enough, because they had not baptism
  Which is the portal of the Faith thou holdest;

And if they were before Christianity,
  In the right manner they adored not God;
  And among such as these am I myself.

For such defects, and not for other guilt,
  Lost are we and are only so far punished,
  That without hope we live on in desire."

Great grief seized on my heart when this I heard,
  Because some people of much worthiness
  I knew, who in that Limbo were suspended.

"Tell me, my Master, tell me, thou my Lord,"
  Began I, with desire of being certain
  Of that Faith which o'ercometh every error,

"Came any one by his own merit hence,
　Or by another's, who was blessed thereafter?"
　And he, who understood my covert speech,

Replied: "I was a novice in this state,
　When I saw hither come a Mighty One,
　With sign of victory incoronate.

Hence he drew forth the shade of the First Parent,
　And that of his son Abel, and of Noah,
　Of Moses the lawgiver, and the obedient

Abraham, patriarch, and David, king,
　Israel with his father and his children,
　And Rachel, for whose sake he did so much,

And others many, and he made them blessed;
　And thou must know, that earlier than these
　Never were any human spirits saved."

We ceased not to advance because he spake,
　But still were passing onward through the forest,
　The forest, say I, of thick-crowded ghosts.

Not very far as yet our way had gone
　This side the summit, when I saw a fire
　That overcame a hemisphere of darkness.

We were a little distant from it still,
　But not so far that I in part discerned not
　That honourable people held that place.

"O thou who honourest every art and science,
　Who may these be, which such great honour have,
　That from the fashion of the rest it parts them?"

And he to me: "The honourable name,
　That sounds of them above there in thy life,
　Wins grace in Heaven, that so advances them."

In the mean time a voice was heard by me:
  "All honour be to the pre-eminent Poet;
  His shade returns again, that was departed."

After the voice had ceased and quiet was,
  Four mighty shades I saw approaching us;
  Semblance had they nor sorrowful nor glad.

To say to me began my gracious Master:
  "Him with that falchion in his hand behold,
  Who comes before the three, even as their lord.

That one is Homer, Poet sovereign;
  He who comes next is Horace, the satirist;
  The third is Ovid, and the last is Lucan.

Because to each of these with me applies
  The name that solitary voice proclaimed,
  They do me honour, and in that do well."

Thus I beheld assemble the fair school
  Of that lord of the song pre-eminent,
  Who o'er the others like an eagle soars.

When they together had discoursed somewhat,
  They turned to me with signs of salutation,
  And on beholding this, my Master smiled;

And more of honour still, much more, they did me,
  In that they made me one of their own band;
  So that the sixth was I, 'mid so much wit.

Thus we went on as far as to the light,
  Things saying 'tis becoming to keep silent,
  As was the saying of them where I was.

We came unto a noble castle's foot,
  Seven times encompassed with lofty walls,
  Defended round by a fair rivulet;

This we passed over even as firm ground;
  Through portals seven I entered with these Sages;
  We came into a meadow of fresh verdure.

People were there with solemn eyes and slow,
  Of great authority in their countenance;
  They spake but seldom, and with gentle voices.

Thus we withdrew ourselves upon one side
  Into an opening luminous and lofty,
  So that they all of them were visible.

There opposite, upon the green enamel,
  Were pointed out to me the mighty spirits,
  Whom to have seen I feel myself exalted.

I saw Electra with companions many,
  'Mongst whom I knew both Hector and Aeneas,
  Caesar in armour with gerfalcon eyes;

I saw Camilla and Penthesilea
  On the other side, and saw the King Latinus,
  Who with Lavinia his daughter sat;

I saw that Brutus who drove Tarquin forth,
  Lucretia, Julia, Marcia, and Cornelia,
  And saw alone, apart, the Saladin.

When I had lifted up my brows a little,
  The Master I beheld of those who know,
  Sit with his philosophic family.

All gaze upon him, and all do him honour.
  There I beheld both Socrates and Plato,
  Who nearer him before the others stand;

Democritus, who puts the world on chance,
  Diogenes, Anaxagoras, and Thales,
  Zeno, Empedocles, and Heraclitus;

Of qualities I saw the good collector,
  Hight Dioscorides; and Orpheus saw I,
  Tully and Livy, and moral Seneca,

Euclid, geometrician, and Ptolemy,
  Galen, Hippocrates, and Avicenna,
  Averroes, who the great Comment made.

I cannot all of them pourtray in full,
  Because so drives me onward the long theme,
  That many times the word comes short of fact.

The sixfold company in two divides;
  Another way my sapient Guide conducts me
  Forth from the quiet to the air that trembles;

And to a place I come where nothing shines.

☙CANTO V

Dante and Virgil descend from the First Circle to the Second. Minos stands at the entrance, judging transgressors and selecting a place in Hell for each of them. The Lustful are eternally tossed upon the "infernal hurricane". Virgil answers Dante's question by describing the shades of famous lovers – Semiramis of Assyria, Dido of Carthage, Helen of Troy, Achilles, Paris, Paolo Malatesta and Francesca Da Rimini. Dante is saddened by the story of the last of these.

Thus I descended out of the first circle
  Down to the second, that less space begirds,
  And so much greater dole, that goads to wailing.

There standeth Minos horribly, and snarls;
  Examines the transgressions at the entrance;
  Judges, and sends according as he girds him.

I say, that when the spirit evil-born
  Cometh before him, wholly it confesses;
  And this discriminator of transgressions

Seeth what place in Hell is meet for it;
  Girds himself with his tail as many times
  As grades he wishes it should be thrust down.

Always before him many of them stand;
  They go by turns each one unto the judgment;
  They speak, and hear, and then are downward hurled.

"O thou, that to this dolorous hostelry
  Comest," said Minos to me, when he saw me,
  Leaving the practice of so great an office,

"Look how thou enterest, and in whom thou trustest;
  Let not the portal's amplitude deceive thee."
  And unto him my Guide: "Why criest thou too?

Do not impede his journey fate-ordained;
  It is so willed there where is power to do
  That which is willed; and ask no further question."

And now begin the dolesome notes to grow
  Audible unto me; now am I come
  There where much lamentation strikes upon me.

I came into a place mute of all light,
  Which bellows as the sea does in a tempest,
  If by opposing winds 'tis combated.

The infernal hurricane that never rests
  Hurtles the spirits onward in its rapine;
  Whirling them round, and smiting, it molests them.

When they arrive before the precipice,
  There are the shrieks, the plaints, and the laments,
  There they blaspheme the puissance divine.

I understood that unto such a torment
  The carnal malefactors were condemned,
  Who reason subjugate to appetite.

And as the wings of starlings bear them on
  In the cold season in large band and full,
  So doth that blast the spirits maledict;

It hither, thither, downward, upward, drives them;
  No hope doth comfort them for evermore,
  Not of repose, but even of lesser pain.

And as the cranes go chanting forth their lays,
  Making in air a long line of themselves,
  So saw I coming, uttering lamentations,

Shadows borne onward by the aforesaid stress.
  Whereupon said I: "Master, who are those
  People, whom the black air so castigates?"

"The first of those, of whom intelligence
  Thou fain wouldst have," then said he unto me,
  "The empress was of many languages.

To sensual vices she was so abandoned,
  That lustful she made licit in her law,
  To remove the blame to which she had been led.

She is Semiramis, of whom we read
  That she succeeded Ninus, and was his spouse;
  She held the land which now the Sultan rules.

The next is she who killed herself for love,
  And broke faith with the ashes of Sichaeus;
  Then Cleopatra the voluptuous."

Helen I saw, for whom so many ruthless
  Seasons revolved; and saw the great Achilles,
  Who at the last hour combated with Love.

Paris I saw, Tristan; and more than a thousand
  Shades did he name and point out with his finger,
  Whom Love had separated from our life.

After that I had listened to my Teacher,
  Naming the dames of eld and cavaliers,
  Pity prevailed, and I was nigh bewildered.

And I began: "O Poet, willingly
  Speak would I to those two, who go together,
  And seem upon the wind to be so light."

And, he to me: "Thou'lt mark, when they shall be
  Nearer to us; and then do thou implore them
  By love which leadeth them, and they will come."

Soon as the wind in our direction sways them,
  My voice uplift I: "O ye weary souls!
  Come speak to us, if no one interdicts it."

As turtle-doves, called onward by desire,
  With open and steady wings to the sweet nest
  Fly through the air by their volition borne,

So came they from the band where Dido is,
  Approaching us athwart the air malign,
  So strong was the affectionate appeal.

"O living creature gracious and benignant,
  Who visiting goest through the purple air
  Us, who have stained the world incarnadine,

If were the King of the Universe our friend,
  We would pray unto him to give thee peace,
  Since thou hast pity on our woe perverse.

Of what it pleases thee to hear and speak,
  That will we hear, and we will speak to you,
  While silent is the wind, as it is now.

Sitteth the city, wherein I was born,
  Upon the sea-shore where the Po descends
  To rest in peace with all his retinue.

Love, that on gentle heart doth swiftly seize,
  Seized this man for the person beautiful
  That was ta'en from me, and still the mode offends me.

Love, that exempts no one beloved from loving,
  Seized me with pleasure of this man so strongly,
  That, as thou seest, it doth not yet desert me;

Love has conducted us unto one death;
  Caina waiteth him who quenched our life!"
  These words were borne along from them to us.

As soon as I had heard those souls tormented,
  I bowed my face, and so long held it down
  Until the Poet said to me: "What thinkest?"

When I made answer, I began: "Alas!
  How many pleasant thoughts, how much desire,
  Conducted these unto the dolorous pass!"

Then unto them I turned me, and I spake,
  And I began: "Thine agonies, Francesca,
  Sad and compassionate to weeping make me.

But tell me, at the time of those sweet sighs,
  By what and in what manner Love conceded,
  That you should know your dubious desires?"

And she to me: "There is no greater sorrow
  Than to be mindful of the happy time
  In misery, and that thy Teacher knows.

But, if to recognise the earliest root
  Of love in us thou hast so great desire,
  I will do even as he who weeps and speaks.

One day we reading were for our delight
  Of Launcelot, how Love did him enthral.
  Alone we were and without any fear.

Full many a time our eyes together drew
  That reading, and drove the colour from our faces;
  But one point only was it that o'ercame us.

When as we read of the much-longed-for smile
  Being by such a noble lover kissed,
  This one, who ne'er from me shall be divided,

Kissed me upon the mouth all palpitating.
  Galeotto was the book and he who wrote it.
  That day no farther did we read therein."

And all the while one spirit uttered this,
  The other one did weep so, that, for pity,
  I swooned away as if I had been dying,

And fell, even as a dead body falls.

❧CANTO VI

*The Gluttons, denizens of the Third Circle, are sunk
in fetid mud and pelted by hail, rain and snow. Virgil
placates the three-headed Cerberus, their bellicose guardian,
by feeding his appetite with fistfuls of earth. Ciacco, a
contemporary of Dante, approaches the pair of travellers
and makes a political prophecy about Florence. Dante asks
Virgil about the Last Judgement as the two poets approach
the next circle.*

At the return of consciousness, that closed
  Before the pity of those two relations,
  Which utterly with sadness had confused me,

New torments I behold, and new tormented
  Around me, whichsoever way I move,
  And whichsoever way I turn, and gaze.

In the third circle am I of the rain
  Eternal, maledict, and cold, and heavy;
  Its law and quality are never new.

Huge hail, and water sombre-hued, and snow,
  Athwart the tenebrous air pour down amain;
  Noisome the earth is, that receiveth this.

Cerberus, monster cruel and uncouth,
  With his three gullets like a dog is barking
  Over the people that are there submerged.

Red eyes he has, and unctuous beard and black,
  And belly large, and armed with claws his hands;
  He rends the spirits, flays, and quarters them.

Howl the rain maketh them like unto dogs;
  One side they make a shelter for the other;
  Oft turn themselves the wretched reprobates.

When Cerberus perceived us, the great worm!
  His mouths he opened, and displayed his tusks;
  Not a limb had he that was motionless.

And my Conductor, with his spans extended,
  Took of the earth, and with his fists well fillèd,
  He threw it into those rapacious gullets.

Such as that dog is, who by barking craves,
  And quiet grows soon as his food he gnaws,
  For to devour it he but thinks and struggles,

The like became those muzzles filth-begrimed
  Of Cerberus the demon, who so thunders
  Over the souls that they would fain be deaf.

We passed across the shadows, which subdues
  The heavy rain-storm, and we placed our feet
  Upon their vanity that person seems.

They all were lying prone upon the earth,
  Excepting one, who sat upright as soon
  As he beheld us passing on before him.

"O thou that art conducted through this Hell,"
  He said to me, "recall me, if thou canst;
  Thyself wast made before I was unmade."

And I to him: "The anguish which thou hast
  Perhaps doth draw thee out of my remembrance,
  So that it seems not I have ever seen thee.

But tell me who thou art, that in so doleful
  A place art put, and in such punishment,
  If some are greater, none is so displeasing."

And he to me: "Thy city, which is full
  Of envy so that now the sack runs over,
  Held me within it in the life serene.

You citizens were wont to call me Ciacco;
  For the pernicious sin of gluttony
  I, as thou seest, am battered by this rain.

And I, sad soul, am not the only one,
  For all these suffer the like penalty
  For the like sin;" and word no more spake he.

I answered him: "Ciacco, thy wretchedness
  Weighs on me so that it to weep invites me;
  But tell me, if thou knowest, to what shall come

The citizens of the divided city;
  If any there be just; and the occasion
  Tell me why so much discord has assailed it."

And he to me: "They, after long contention,
  Will come to bloodshed; and the rustic party
  Will drive the other out with much offence.

Then afterwards behoves it this one fall
  Within three suns, and rise again the other
  By force of him who now is on the coast.

High will it hold its forehead a long while,
  Keeping the other under heavy burdens,
  Howe'er it weeps thereat and is indignant.

The just are two, and are not understood there;
  Envy and Arrogance and Avarice
  Are the three sparks that have all hearts enkindled."

Here ended he his tearful utterance;
  And I to him: "I wish thee still to teach me,
  And make a gift to me of further speech.

Farinata and Tegghiaio, once so worthy,
  Jacopo Rusticucci, Arrigo and Mosca,
  And others who on good deeds set their thoughts,

Say where they are, and cause that I may know them;
  For great desire constraineth me to learn
  If Heaven doth sweeten them, or Hell envenom."

And he: "They are among the blacker souls;
  A different sin downweighs them to the bottom;
  If thou so far descendest, thou canst see them.

But when thou art again in the sweet world,
  I pray thee to the mind of others bring me;
  No more I tell thee and no more I answer."

Then his straightforward eyes he turned askance,
  Eyed me a little, and then bowed his head;
  He fell therewith prone like the other blind.

And the Guide said to me: "He wakes no more
  This side the sound of the angelic trumpet;
  When shall approach the hostile Potentate,

Each one shall find again his dismal tomb,
  Shall reassume his flesh and his own figure,
  Shall hear what through eternity re-echoes."

So we passed onward o'er the filthy mixture
  Of shadows and of rain with footsteps slow,
  Touching a little on the future life.

Wherefore I said: "Master, these torments here,
  Will they increase after the mighty sentence,
  Or lesser be, or will they be as burning?"

And he to me: "Return unto thy science,
  Which wills, that as the thing more perfect is,
  The more it feels of pleasure and of pain.

Albeit that this people maledict
  To true perfection never can attain,
  Hereafter more than now they look to be."

Round in a circle by that road we went,
  Speaking much more, which I do not repeat;
  We came unto the point where the descent is;

There we found Plutus the great enemy.

‚CANTO VII

*At Virgil's behest, Plutus, god of material wealth, dissipates
into thin air between the Third and Fourth Circles. The
poets watch the noisy Hoarders and the Spendthrifts rolling
huge weights at one another. After discussing Fortune's
distribution of temporal riches, they reach the river Styx,
the second of Hell's rivers, which is the Fifth Circle. Here
are mired the Wrathful, who tear at one another, and the
Sluggish, who doze beneath the slime. Dante and Virgil
come to the foot of a high tower.*

"*Pape Satan, Pape Satan, Aleppe!*"
  Thus Plutus with his clucking voice began;
  And that benignant Sage, who all things knew,

Said, to encourage me: "Let not thy fear
  Harm thee; for any power that he may have
  Shall not prevent thy going down this crag."

Then he turned round unto that bloated lip,
  And said: "Be silent, thou accursed wolf;
  Consume within thyself with thine own rage.

Not causeless is this journey to the abyss;
  Thus is it willed on high, where Michael wrought
  Vengeance upon the proud adultery."

Even as the sails inflated by the wind
  Involved together fall when snaps the mast,
  So fell the cruel monster to the earth.

Thus we descended into the fourth chasm,
  Gaining still farther on the dolesome shore
  Which all the woe of the universe insacks.

Justice of God, ah! Who heaps up so many
  New toils and sufferings as I beheld?
  And why doth our transgression waste us so?

As doth the billow there upon Charybdis,
  That breaks itself on that which it encounters,
  So here the folk must dance their roundelay.

Here saw I people, more than elsewhere, many,
  On one side and the other, with great howls,
  Rolling weights forward by main force of chest.

They clashed together, and then at that point
  Each one turned backward, rolling retrograde,
  Crying, "Why keepest?" and, "Why squanderest thou?"

Thus they returned along the lurid circle
  On either hand unto the opposite point,
  Shouting their shameful metre evermore.

Then each, when he arrived there, wheeled about
  Through his half-circle to another joust;
  And I, who had my heart pierced as it were,

Exclaimed: "My Master, now declare to me
  What people these are, and if all were clerks,
  These shaven crowns upon the left of us."

And he to me: "All of them were asquint
  In intellect in the first life, so much
  That there with measure they no spending made.

Clearly enough their voices bark it forth,
  Whene'er they reach the two points of the circle,
  Where sunders them the opposite defect.

Clerks those were who no hairy covering
  Have on the head, and Popes and Cardinals,
  In whom doth Avarice practise its excess."

And I: "My Master, among such as these
  I ought forsooth to recognise some few,
  Who were infected with these maladies."

And he to me: "Vain thought thou entertainest;
  The undiscerning life which made them sordid
  Now makes them unto all discernment dim.

Forever shall they come to these two buttings;
  These from the sepulchre shall rise again
  With the fist closed, and these with tresses shorn.

Ill giving and ill keeping the fair world
  Have ta'en from them, and placed them in this scuffle;
  Whate'er it be, no words adorn I for it.

Now canst thou, Son, behold the transient farce
  Of goods that are committed unto Fortune,
  For which the human race each other buffet;

For all the gold that is beneath the moon,
  Or ever has been, of these weary souls
  Could never make a single one repose."

"Master," I said to him, "now tell me also
  What is this Fortune which thou speakest of,
  That has the world's goods so within its clutches?"

And he to me: "O creatures imbecile,
  What ignorance is this which doth beset you?
  Now will I have thee learn my judgment of her.

He whose omniscience everything transcends
  The heavens created, and gave who should guide them,
  That every part to every part may shine,

Distributing the light in equal measure;
  He in like manner to the mundane splendours
  Ordained a general ministress and guide,

That she might change at times the empty treasures
  From race to race, from one blood to another,
  Beyond resistance of all human wisdom.

Therefore one people triumphs, and another
  Languishes, in pursuance of her judgment,
  Which hidden is, as in the grass a serpent.

Your knowledge has no counterstand against her;
  She makes provision, judges, and pursues
  Her governance, as theirs the other gods.

Her permutations have not any truce;
  Necessity makes her precipitate,
  So often cometh who his turn obtains.

And this is she who is so crucified
  Even by those who ought to give her praise,
  Giving her blame amiss, and bad repute.

But she is blissful, and she hears it not;
  Among the other primal creatures gladsome
  She turns her sphere, and blissful she rejoices.

Let us descend now unto greater woe;
  Already sinks each star that was ascending
  When I set out, and loitering is forbidden."

We crossed the circle to the other bank,
  Near to a fount that boils, and pours itself
  Along a gully that runs out of it.

The water was more sombre far than perse;
  And we, in company with the dusky waves,
  Made entrance downward by a path uncouth.

A marsh it makes, which has the name of Styx,
  This tristful brooklet, when it has descended
  Down to the foot of the malign grey shores.

And I, who stood intent upon beholding,
  Saw people mud-besprent in that lagoon,
  All of them naked and with angry look.

They smote each other not alone with hands,
  But with the head and with the breast and feet,
  Tearing each other piecemeal with their teeth.

Said the good Master: "Son, thou now beholdest
  The souls of those whom anger overcame;
  And likewise I would have thee know for certain

Beneath the water people are who sigh
  And make this water bubble at the surface,
  As the eye tells thee wheresoe'er it turns.

Fixed in the mire they say, 'We sullen were
  In the sweet air, which by the sun is gladdened,
  Bearing within ourselves the sluggish reek;

Now we are sullen in this sable mire.'
  This hymn do they keep gurgling in their throats,
  For with unbroken words they cannot say it."

Thus we went circling round the filthy fen
  A great arc 'twixt the dry bank and the swamp,
  With eyes turned unto those who gorge the mire;

Unto the foot of a tower we came at last.

❧CANTO VIII

Dante realizes that the fires on top of the tower are a signal to the city of Dis. Phlegyas quickly appears and the two poets are ferried across the Styx. An angry shadow, Philippo Argenti, rises up from the mire and tries to attack the boat. Repelled by Virgil, he is then viciously attacked by the other souls. The poets disembark at the gate of Dis. They are denied access by the demonic angels within. Virgil goes alone to speak with them, to no avail. The poets must wait for help from Heaven.

I say, continuing, that long before
 We to the foot of that high tower had come,
 Our eyes went upward to the summit of it,

By reason of two flamelets we saw placed there,
 And from afar another answer them,
 So far, that hardly could the eye attain it.

And, to the sea of all discernment turned,
 I said: "What sayeth this, and what respondeth
 That other fire? And who are they that made it?"

And he to me: "Across the turbid waves
 What is expected thou canst now discern,
 If reek of the morass conceal it not."

Cord never shot an arrow from itself
 That sped away athwart the air so swift,
 As I beheld a very little boat

Come o'er the water tow'rds us at that moment,
 Under the guidance of a single pilot,
 Who shouted, "Now art thou arrived, fell soul?"

"Phlegyas, Phlegyas, thou criest out in vain
  For this once," said my Lord; "thou shalt not have us
  Longer than in the passing of the slough."

As he who listens to some great deceit
  That has been done to him, and then resents it,
  Such became Phlegyas, in his gathered wrath.

My Guide descended down into the boat,
  And then he made me enter after him,
  And only when I entered seemed it laden.

Soon as the Guide and I were in the boat,
  The antique prow goes on its way, dividing
  More of the water than 'tis wont with others.

While we were running through the dead canal,
  Uprose in front of me one full of mire,
  And said, "Who'rt thou that comest ere the hour?"

And I to him: "Although I come, I stay not;
  But who art thou that hast become so squalid?"
  "Thou seest that I am one who weeps," he answered.

And I to him: "With weeping and with wailing,
  Thou spirit maledict, do thou remain;
  For thee I know, though thou art all defiled."

Then stretched he both his hands unto the boat;
  Whereat my wary Master thrust him back,
  Saying, "Away there with the other dogs!"

Thereafter with his arms he clasped my neck;
  He kissed my face, and said: "Disdainful soul,
  Blessed be she who bore thee in her bosom.

That was an arrogant person in the world;
  Goodness is none, that decks his memory;
  So likewise here his shade is furious.

How many are esteemed great kings up there,
  Who here shall be like unto swine in mire,
  Leaving behind them horrible dispraises!"

And I: "My Master, much should I be pleased,
  If I could see him soused into this broth,
  Before we issue forth out of the lake."

And he to me: "Ere unto thee the shore
  Reveal itself, thou shalt be satisfied;
  Such a desire 'tis meet thou shouldst enjoy."

A little after that, I saw such havoc
  Made of him by the people of the mire,
  That still I praise and thank my God for it.

They all were shouting, "At Philippo Argenti!"
  And that exasperate spirit Florentine
  Turned round upon himself with his own teeth.

We left him there, and more of him I tell not;
  But on mine ears there smote a lamentation,
  Whence forward I intent unbar mine eyes.

And the good Master said: "Even now, my Son,
  The city draweth near whose name is Dis,
  With the grave citizens, with the great throng."

And I: "Its mosques already, Master, clearly
  Within there in the valley I discern
  Vermilion, as if issuing from the fire

They were." And he to me: "The fire eternal
  That kindles them within makes them look red,
  As thou beholdest in this nether Hell."

Then we arrived within the moats profound,
  That circumvallate that disconsolate city;
  The walls appeared to me to be of iron.

Not without making first a circuit wide,
  We came unto a place where loud the pilot
  Cried out to us, "Debark, here is the entrance."

More than a thousand at the gates I saw
  Out of the Heavens rained down, who angrily
  Were saying, "Who is this that without death

Goes through the kingdom of the people dead?"
  And my sagacious Master made a sign
  Of wishing secretly to speak with them.

A little then they quelled their great disdain,
  And said: "Come thou alone, and he begone
  Who has so boldly entered these dominions.

Let him return alone by his mad road;
  Try, if he can; for thou shalt here remain,
  Who hast escorted him through such dark regions."

Think, Reader, if I was discomforted
  At utterance of the accursed words;
  For never to return here I believed.

"O my dear Guide, who more than seven times
  Hast rendered me security, and drawn me
  From imminent peril that before me stood,

Do not desert me," said I, "thus undone;
  And if the going farther be denied us,
  Let us retrace our steps together swiftly."

And that Lord, who had led me thitherward,
  Said unto me: "Fear not; because our passage
  None can take from us, it by Such is given.

But here await me, and thy weary spirit
  Comfort and nourish with a better hope;
  For in this nether world I will not leave thee."

So onward goes and there abandons me
　My Father sweet, and I remain in doubt,
　For No and Yes within my head contend.

I could not hear what he proposed to them;
　But with them there he did not linger long,
　Ere each within in rivalry ran back.

They closed the portals, those our adversaries,
　On my Lord's breast, who had remained without
　And turned to me with footsteps far between.

His eyes cast down, his forehead shorn had he
　Of all its boldness, and he said, with sighs,
　"Who has denied to me the dolesome houses?"

And unto me: "Thou, because I am angry,
　Fear not, for I will conquer in the trial,
　Whatever for defence within be planned.

This arrogance of theirs is nothing new;
　For once they used it at less secret gate,
　Which finds itself without a fastening still.

O'er it didst thou behold the dead inscription;
　And now this side of it descends the steep,
　Passing across the circles without escort,

One by whose means the city shall be opened."

⤳CANTO IX

The poets are waiting for Divine assistance at the gate of Dis. Unnerved by Virgil's anxiety, Dante asks him if he knows the way through Hell. Virgil reassures him. Three Furies appear at the tower, shrieking and tearing at their breasts and invoking Medusa. Dante shields his gaze to avoid being turned to stone. An angel makes a dramatic entrance before opening the gate. The sarcophagi of the groaning Heretics burn beyond.

That hue which cowardice brought out on me,
  Beholding my Conductor backward turn,
  Sooner repressed within him his new colour.

He stopped attentive, like a man who listens,
  Because the eye could not conduct him far
  Through the black air, and through the heavy fog.

"Still it behoveth us to win the fight,"
  Began he: "Else. . . such offered us herself. . .
  O how I long that some one here arrive!"

Well I perceived, as soon as the beginning
  He covered up with what came afterward,
  That they were words quite different from the first;

But none the less his saying gave me fear,
  Because I carried out the broken phrase,
  Perhaps to a worse meaning than he had.

"Into this bottom of the doleful conch
  Doth any e'er descend from the first grade,
  Which for its pain has only hope cut off?"

This question put I; and he answered me:
  "Seldom it comes to pass that one of us
  Maketh the journey upon which I go.

True is it, once before I here below
   Was conjured by that pitiless Erictho,
   Who summoned back the shades unto their bodies.

Naked of me short while the flesh had been,
   Before within that wall she made me enter,
   To bring a spirit from the circle of Judas;

That is the lowest region and the darkest,
   And farthest from the heaven which circles all.
   Well know I the way; therefore be reassured.

This fen, which a prodigious stench exhales,
   Encompasses about the city dolent,
   Where now we cannot enter without anger."

And more he said, but not in mind I have it;
   Because mine eye had altogether drawn me
   Tow'rds the high tower with the red-flaming summit,

Where in a moment saw I swift uprisen
   The three infernal Furies stained with blood,
   Who had the limbs of women and their mien,

And with the greenest hydras were begirt;
   Small serpents and cerastes were their tresses,
   Wherewith their horrid temples were entwined.

And he who well the handmaids of the Queen
   Of everlasting lamentation knew,
   Said unto me: "Behold the fierce Erinnys.

This is Megaera, on the left-hand side;
   She who is weeping on the right, Alecto;
   Tisiphone is between;" and then was silent.

Each one her breast was rending with her nails;
   They beat them with their palms, and cried so loud,
   That I for dread pressed close unto the Poet.

"Medusa come, so we to stone will change him!"
  All shouted looking down: "In evil hour
  Avenged we not on Theseus his assault!"

"Turn thyself round, and keep thine eyes close shut,
  For if the Gorgon appear, and thou shouldst see it,
  No more returning upward would there be."

Thus said the Master; and he turned me round
  Himself, and trusted not unto my hands
  So far as not to blind me with his own.

O ye who have undistempered intellects,
  Observe the doctrine that conceals itself
  Beneath the veil of the mysterious verses!

And now there came across the turbid waves
  The clangour of a sound with terror fraught,
  Because of which both of the margins trembled;

Not otherwise it was than of a wind
  Impetuous on account of adverse heats,
  That smites the forest, and, without restraint,

The branches rends, beats down, and bears away;
  Right onward, laden with dust, it goes superb,
  And puts to flight the wild beasts and the shepherds.

Mine eyes he loosed, and said: "Direct the nerve
  Of vision now along that ancient foam,
  There yonder where that smoke is most intense."

Even as the frogs before the hostile serpent
  Across the water scatter all abroad,
  Until each one is huddled in the earth.

More than a thousand ruined souls I saw,
  Thus fleeing from before one who on foot
  Was passing o'er the Styx with soles unwet.

From off his face he fanned that unctuous air,
  Waving his left hand oft in front of him,
  And only with that anguish seemed he weary.

Well I perceived one sent from Heaven was he,
  And to the Master turned; and he made sign
  That I should quiet stand, and bow before him.

Ah! how disdainful he appeared to me!
  He reached the gate, and with a little rod
  He opened it, for there was no resistance.

"O banished out of Heaven, people despised!"
  Thus he began upon the horrid threshold;
  "Whence is this arrogance within you couched?

Wherefore recalcitrate against that will,
  From which the end can never be cut off,
  And which has many times increased your pain?

What helpeth it to butt against the fates?
  Your Cerberus, if you remember well,
  For that still bears his chin and gullet peeled."

Then he returned along the miry road,
  And spake no word to us, but had the look
  Of one whom other care constrains and goads

Than that of him who in his presence is;
  And we our feet directed tow'rds the city,
  After those holy words all confident.

Within we entered without any contest;
  And I, who inclination had to see
  What the condition such a fortress holds,

Soon as I was within, cast round mine eye,
  And see on every hand an ample plain,
  Full of distress and torment terrible.

Even as at Arles, where stagnant grows the Rhone,
  Even as at Pola near to the Quarnaro,
  That shuts in Italy and bathes its borders,

The sepulchres make all the place uneven;
  So likewise did they there on every side,
  Saving that there the manner was more bitter;

For flames between the sepulchres were scattered,
  By which they so intensely heated were,
  That iron more so asks not any art.

All of their coverings uplifted were,
  And from them issued forth such dire laments,
  Sooth seemed they of the wretched and tormented.

And I: "My Master, what are all those people
  Who, having sepulture within those tombs,
  Make themselves audible by doleful sighs?"

And he to me: "Here are the Heresiarchs,
  With their disciples of all sects, and much
  More than thou thinkest laden are the tombs.

Here like together with its like is buried;
  And more and less the monuments are heated."
  And when he to the right had turned, we passed

Between the torments and high parapets.

CANTO X

Dante and Virgil walk around the tombs of the Heretics who sought temporal bliss. This sin of the intellect, though not a source of sinful action, lies between Incontinence and Violence. Hearing a fellow Tuscan speak, Farinata rises up from one of the graves. Farinata's political tirade against Florence is interrupted by the appearance of Cavalcante De' Cavalcanti, who asks about his son Guido. Dante is intrigued to discover that the damned can foresee the future and recall the past but have no knowledge of the present.

Now onward goes, along a narrow path
  Between the torments and the city wall,
  My Master, and I follow at his back.

"O power supreme, that through these impious circles
  Turnest me," I began, "as pleases thee,
  Speak to me, and my longings satisfy;

The people who are lying in these tombs,
  Might they be seen? Already are uplifted
  The covers all, and no one keepeth guard."

And he to me: "They all will be closed up
  When from Jehoshaphat they shall return
  Here with the bodies they have left above.

Their cemetery have upon this side
  With Epicurus all his followers,
  Who with the body mortal make the soul;

But in the question thou dost put to me,
  Within here shalt thou soon be satisfied,
  And likewise in the wish thou keepest silent."

And I: "Good Leader, I but keep concealed
  From thee my heart, that I may speak the less,
  Nor only now hast thou thereto disposed me."

"O Tuscan, thou who through the city of fire
  Goest alive, thus speaking modestly,
  Be pleased to stay thy footsteps in this place.

Thy mode of speaking makes thee manifest
  A native of that noble fatherland,
  To which perhaps I too molestful was."

Upon a sudden issued forth this sound
  From out one of the tombs; wherefore I pressed,
  Fearing, a little nearer to my Leader.

And unto me he said: "Turn thee; what dost thou?
  Behold there Farinata who has risen;
  From the waist upwards wholly shalt thou see him."

I had already fixed mine eyes on his,
  And he uprose erect with breast and front
  E'en as if Hell he had in great despite.

And with courageous hands and prompt my Leader
  Thrust me between the sepulchres towards him,
  Exclaiming, "Let thy words explicit be."

As soon as I was at the foot of his tomb
  Somewhat he eyed me, and, as if disdainful,
  Then asked of me, "Who were thine ancestors?"

I, who desirous of obeying was,
  Concealed it not, but all revealed to him;
  Whereat he raised his brows a little upward.

Then said he: "Fiercely adverse have they been
  To me, and to my fathers, and my party;
  So that two several times I scattered them."

"If they were banished, they returned on all sides,"
  I answered him, "the first time and the second;
  But yours have not acquired that art aright."

Then there uprose upon the sight, uncovered
  Down to the chin, a shadow at his side;
  I think that he had risen on his knees.

Round me he gazed, as if solicitude
  He had to see if some one else were with me,
  But after his suspicion was all spent,

Weeping, he said to me: "If through this blind
  Prison thou goest by loftiness of genius,
  Where is my son? And why is he not with thee?"

And I to him: "I come not of myself;
  He who is waiting yonder leads me here,
  Whom in disdain perhaps your Guido had."

His language and the mode of punishment
  Already unto me had read his name;
  On that account my answer was so full.

Up starting suddenly, he cried out: "How
  Saidst thou – he had? Is he not still alive?
  Does not the sweet light strike upon his eyes?"

When he became aware of some delay,
  Which I before my answer made, supine
  He fell again, and forth appeared no more.

But the other, magnanimous, at whose desire
  I had remained, did not his aspect change,
  Neither his neck he moved, nor bent his side.

"And if," continuing his first discourse,
  "They have that art," he said, "not learned aright,
  That more tormenteth me, than doth this bed.

But fifty times shall not rekindled be
  The countenance of the Lady who reigns here,
  Ere thou shalt know how heavy is that art;

And as thou wouldst to the sweet world return,
  Say why that people is so pitiless
  Against my race in each one of its laws?"

Whence I to him: "The slaughter and great carnage
  Which have with crimson stained the Arbia, cause
  Such orisons in our temple to be made."

After his head he with a sigh had shaken,
  "There I was not alone," he said, "nor surely
  Without a cause had with the others moved.

But there I was alone, where every one
  Consented to the laying waste of Florence,
  He who defended her with open face."

"Ah! So hereafter may your seed repose,"
  I him entreated, "solve for me that knot,
  Which has entangled my conceptions here.

It seems that you can see, if I hear rightly,
  Beforehand whatsoe'er time brings with it,
  And in the present have another mode."

"We see, like those who have imperfect sight,
  The things", he said, "that distant are from us;
  So much still shines on us the Sovereign Ruler.

When they draw near, or are, is wholly vain
  Our intellect, and if none brings it to us,
  Not anything know we of your human state.

Hence thou canst understand, that wholly dead
  Will be our knowledge from the moment when
  The portal of the future shall be closed."

Then I, as if compunctious for my fault,
  Said: "Now, then, you will tell that fallen one,
  That still his son is with the living joined.

And if just now, in answering, I was dumb,
  Tell him I did it because I was thinking
  Already of the error you have solved me."

And now my Master was recalling me,
  Wherefore more eagerly I prayed the spirit
  That he would tell me who was with him there.

He said: "With more than a thousand here I lie;
  Within here is the second Frederick,
  And the Cardinal, and of the rest I speak not."

Thereon he hid himself; and I towards
  The ancient poet turned my steps, reflecting
  Upon that saying, which seemed hostile to me.

He moved along; and afterward thus going,
  He said to me, "Why art thou so bewildered?"
  And I in his inquiry satisfied him.

"Let memory preserve what thou hast heard
  Against thyself," that Sage commanded me,
  "And now attend here;" and he raised his finger.

"When thou shalt be before the radiance sweet
  Of her whose beauteous eyes all things behold,
  From her thou'lt know the journey of thy life."

Unto the left hand then he turned his feet;
  We left the wall, and went towards the middle,
  Along a path that strikes into a valley,

Which even up there unpleasant made its stench.

❧CANTO XI

Continuing their visit of the heretical Sixth Circle, poet and pilgrim are overcome by the foul stench wafting up from the abyss ahead. Both pause and read the inscription on the tomb of Pope Anastasius II. Seeing Dante's willingness to learn, Virgil instructs him further on the subtle classification of punishment in Hell before finally urging him on as it is nearly dawn.

Upon the margin of a lofty bank
  Which great rocks broken in a circle made,
  We came upon a still more cruel throng;

And there, by reason of the horrible
  Excess of stench the deep abyss throws out,
  We drew ourselves aside behind the cover

Of a great tomb, whereon I saw a writing,
  Which said: "Pope Anastasius I hold,
  Whom out of the right way Photinus drew."

"Slow it behoveth our descent to be,
  So that the sense be first a little used
  To the sad blast, and then we shall not heed it."

The Master thus; and unto him I said,
  "Some compensation find, that the time pass not
  Idly;" and he: "Thou seest I think of that.

My son, upon the inside of these rocks",
  Began he then to say, "are three small circles,
  From grade to grade, like those which thou art leaving.

They all are full of spirits maledict;
  But that hereafter sight alone suffice thee,
  Hear how and wherefore they are in constraint.

Of every malice that wins hate in Heaven,
  Injury is the end; and all such end
  Either by force or fraud afflicteth others.

But because fraud is man's peculiar vice,
  More it displeases God; and so stand lowest
  The fraudulent, and greater dole assails them.

All the first circle of the Violent is;
  But since force may be used against three persons,
  In three rounds 'tis divided and constructed.

To God, to ourselves, and to our neighbour can we
  Use force; I say on them and on their things,
  As thou shalt hear with reason manifest.

A death by violence, and painful wounds,
  Are to our neighbour given; and in his substance
  Ruin, and arson, and injurious levies;

Whence homicides, and he who smites unjustly,
  Marauders, and freebooters, the first round
  Tormenteth all in companies diverse.

Man may lay violent hands upon himself
  And his own goods; and therefore in the second
  Round must perforce without avail repent

Whoever of your world deprives himself,
  Who games, and dissipates his property,
  And weepeth there, where he should jocund be.

Violence can be done the Deity,
  In heart denying and blaspheming Him,
  And by disdaining Nature and her bounty.

And for this reason doth the smallest round
  Seal with its signet Sodom and Cahors,
  And who, disdaining God, speaks from the heart.

Fraud, wherewithal is every conscience stung,
  A man may practise upon him who trusts,
  And him who doth no confidence imburse.

This latter mode, it would appear, dissevers
  Only the bond of love which Nature makes;
  Wherefore within the second circle nestle

Hypocrisy, flattery and who deals in magic,
  Falsification, theft and simony,
  Panders, and barrators, and the like filth.

By the other mode, forgotten is that love
  Which Nature makes, and what is after added,
  From which there is a special faith engendered.

Hence in the smallest circle, where the point is
  Of the Universe, upon which Dis is seated,
  Whoe'er betrays for ever is consumed."

And I: "My Master, clear enough proceeds
  Thy reasoning, and full well distinguishes
  This cavern and the people who possess it.

But tell me, those within the fat lagoon,
  Whom the wind drives, and whom the rain doth beat,
  And who encounter with such bitter tongues,

Wherefore are they inside of the red city
  Not punished, if God has them in his wrath,
  And if he has not, wherefore in such fashion?"

And unto me he said: "Why wanders so
  Thine intellect from that which it is wont?
  Or, sooth, thy mind where is it elsewhere looking?

Hast thou no recollection of those words
  With which thine Ethics thoroughly discusses
  The dispositions three, that Heaven abides not –

Incontinence, and Malice, and insane
    Bestiality? And how Incontinence
    Less God offendeth, and less blame attracts?

If thou regardest this conclusion well,
    And to thy mind recallest who they are
    That up outside are undergoing penance,

Clearly wilt thou perceive why from these felons
    They separated are, and why less wroth
    Justice divine doth smite them with its hammer."

"O Sun, that healest all distempered vision,
    Thou dost content me so, when thou resolvest,
    That doubting pleases me no less than knowing!

Once more a little backward turn thee," said I,
    "There where thou sayest that usury offends
    Goodness divine, and disengage the knot."

"Philosophy," he said, "to him who heeds it,
    Noteth, not only in one place alone,
    After what manner Nature takes her course

From Intellect Divine, and from its art;
    And if thy Physics carefully thou notest,
    After not many pages shalt thou find,

That this your art as far as possible
    Follows, as the disciple doth the master;
    So that your art is, as it were, God's grandchild.

From these two, if thou bringest to thy mind
    Genesis at the beginning, it behoves
    Mankind to gain their life and to advance;

And since the usurer takes another way,
    Nature herself and in her follower
    Disdains he, for elsewhere he puts his hope.

But follow, now, as I would fain go on,
  For quivering are the Fishes on the horizon,
  And the Wain wholly over Caurus lies,

And far beyond there we descend the crag."

⮦CANTO XII

Dante and Virgil enter the Seventh Circle by means of a
landslide created by Christ when he harrowed Hell. The
Minotaur, guardian of the Violent, breaks into a fit of
rage on seeing the poets. Fleeing past him, the poets reach
Phlegethon, a river of boiling blood that is filled with those
that have inflicted violence on others. Three fierce Centaurs
shoot arrows at souls attempting to rise above the level
commensurate with their punishment. Virgil asks Chiron,
their leader, to lend one of his band to them, so that they
might ford the river. Nessus is chosen, who points out
sinners along the way.

The place where to descend the bank we came
  Was alpine, and from what was there, moreover,
  Of such a kind that every eye would shun it.

Such as that ruin is which in the flank
  Smote, on this side of Trent, the Adige,
  Either by earthquake or by failing stay,

For from the mountain's top, from which it moved,
  Unto the plain the cliff is shattered so,
  Some path 'twould give to him who was above;

Even such was the descent of that ravine,
  And on the border of the broken chasm
  The infamy of Crete was stretched along,

Who was conceived in the fictitious cow;
  And when he us beheld, he bit himself,
  Even as one whom anger racks within.

My Sage towards him shouted: "Peradventure
  Thou think'st that here may be the Duke of Athens,
  Who in the world above brought death to thee?

Get thee gone, beast, for this one cometh not
  Instructed by thy sister, but he comes
  In order to behold your punishments."

As is that bull who breaks loose at the moment
  In which he has received the mortal blow,
  Who cannot walk, but staggers here and there,

The Minotaur beheld I do the like;
  And he, the wary, cried: "Run to the passage;
  While he wroth, 'tis well thou shouldst descend."

Thus down we took our way o'er that discharge
  Of stones, which oftentimes did move themselves
  Beneath my feet, from the unwonted burden.

Thoughtful I went; and he said: "Thou art thinking
  Perhaps upon this ruin, which is guarded
  By that brute anger which just now I quenched.

Now will I have thee know, the other time
  I here descended to the nether Hell,
  This precipice had not yet fallen down.

But truly, if I well discern, a little
  Before His coming who the mighty spoil
  Bore off from Dis, in the supernal circle,

Upon all sides the deep and loathsome valley
  Trembled so, that I thought the Universe
  Was thrilled with love, by which there are who think

The world ofttimes converted into chaos;
  And at that moment this primeval crag
  Both here and elsewhere made such overthrow.

But fix thine eyes below; for draweth near
  The river of blood, within which boiling is
  Whoe'er by violence doth injure others."

O blind cupidity, O wrath insane,
  That spurs us onward so in our short life,
  And in the eternal then so badly steeps us!

I saw an ample moat bent like a bow,
  As one which all the plain encompasses,
  Conformable to what my Guide had said.

And between this and the embankment's foot
  Centaurs in file were running, armed with arrows,
  As in the world they used the chase to follow.

Beholding us descend, each one stood still,
  And from the squadron three detached themselves,
  With bows and arrows in advance selected;

And from afar one cried: "Unto what torment
  Come ye, who down the hillside are descending?
  Tell us from there; if not, I draw the bow."

My Master said: "Our answer will we make
  To Chiron, near you there; in evil hour,
  That will of thine was evermore so hasty."

Then touched he me, and said: "This one is Nessus,
  Who perished for the lovely Dejanira,
  And for himself, himself did vengeance take.

And he in the midst, who at his breast is gazing,
  Is the great Chiron, who brought up Achilles;
  That other Pholus is, who was so wrathful.

Thousands and thousands go about the moat
  Shooting with shafts whatever soul emerges
  Out of the blood, more than his crime allots."

Near we approached unto those monsters fleet;
  Chiron an arrow took, and with the notch
  Backward upon his jaws he put his beard.

After he had uncovered his great mouth,
  He said to his companions: "Are you ware
  That he behind moveth whate'er he touches?

Thus are not wont to do the feet of dead men."
  And my good Guide, who now was at his breast,
  Where the two natures are together joined,

Replied: "Indeed he lives, and thus alone
  Me it behoves to show him the dark valley;
  Necessity, and not delight, impels us.

Some one withdrew from singing Halleluja,
  Who unto me committed this new office;
  No thief is he, nor I a thievish spirit.

But by that virtue through which I am moving
  My steps along this savage thoroughfare,
  Give us some one of thine, to be with us,

And who may show us where to pass the ford,
  And who may carry this one on his back;
  For 'tis no spirit that can walk the air."

Upon his right breast Chiron wheeled about,
  And said to Nessus: "Turn and do thou guide them,
  And warn aside, if other band may meet you."

We with our faithful escort onward moved
  Along the brink of the vermilion boiling,
  Wherein the boiled were uttering loud laments.

People I saw within up to the eyebrows,
  And the great Centaur said: "Tyrants are these,
  Who dealt in bloodshed and in pillaging.

Here they lament their pitiless mischiefs; here
  Is Alexander, and fierce Dionysius
  Who upon Sicily brought dolorous years.

That forehead there which has the hair so black
  Is Azzolin; and the other who is blond,
  Obizzo is of Esti, who, in truth,

Up in the world was by his stepson slain."
  Then turned I to the Poet; and he said,
  "Now he be first to thee, and second I."

A little farther on the Centaur stopped
  Above a folk, who far down as the throat
  Seemed from that boiling stream to issue forth.

A shade he showed us on one side alone,
  Saying: "He cleft asunder in God's bosom
  The heart that still upon the Thames is honoured."

Then people saw I, who from out the river
  Lifted their heads and also all the chest;
  And many among these I recognised.

Thus ever more and more grew shallower
  That blood, so that the feet alone it covered;
  And there across the moat our passage was.

"Even as thou here upon this side beholdest
  The boiling stream, that aye diminishes,"
  The Centaur said, "I wish thee to believe

That on this other more and more declines
  Its bed, until it reunites itself
  Where it behoveth tyranny to groan.

Justice divine, upon this side, is goading
  That Attila, who was a scourge on Earth,
  And Pyrrhus, and Sextus; and for ever milks

The tears which with the boiling it unseals
  In Rinier da Corneto and Rinier Pazzo,
  Who made upon the highways so much war."

Then back he turned, and passed again the ford.

∾CANTO XIII

The swift passage across the third river of Hell plunges the visitors into the thick Wood of the Suicides who are denied bodily form. Dante breaks off a branch from a nearby tree. It weeps blood and speaks. This wretch was once Pier delle Vigne, chief adviser to Frederick II of Sicily, who explains that he and other sinners like him suffer indescribable torment when the half-bird, half-beast harpies rend their bark. This exchange is interrupted by two Profligates, Lano of Siena and Giacomo da Sant'Andrea, who are being pursued by hounds. One of them gets torn to pieces by the creatures. The poets speak to a Florentine, who is now a weeping bush.

Not yet had Nessus reached the other side,
  When we had put ourselves within a wood,
  That was not marked by any path whatever.

Not foliage green, but of a dusky colour,
  Not branches smooth, but gnarled and intertangled,
  Not apple-trees were there, but thorns with poison.

Such tangled thickets have not, nor so dense,
  Those savage wild beasts, that in hatred hold
  'Twixt Cecina and Corneto the tilled places.

There do the hideous Harpies make their nests,
  Who chased the Trojans from the Strophades,
  With sad announcement of impending doom;

Broad wings have they, and necks and faces human,
  And feet with claws, and their great bellies fledged;
  They make laments upon the wondrous trees.

And the good Master: "Ere thou enter farther,
  Know that thou art within the second round,"
  Thus he began to say, "and shalt be, till

Thou comest out upon the horrible sand;
  Therefore look well around, and thou shalt see
  Things that will credence give unto my speech."

I heard on all sides lamentations uttered,
  And person none beheld I who might make them,
  Whence, utterly bewildered, I stood still.

I think he thought that I perhaps might think
  So many voices issued through those trunks
  From people who concealed themselves from us;

Therefore the Master said: "If thou break off
  Some little spray from any of these trees,
  The thoughts thou hast will wholly be made vain."

Then stretched I forth my hand a little forward,
  And plucked a branchlet off from a great thorn;
  And the trunk cried, "Why dost thou mangle me?"

After it had become embrowned with blood,
  It recommenced its cry: "Why dost thou rend me?
  Hast thou no spirit of pity whatsoever?

Men once we were, and now are changed to trees;
  Indeed, thy hand should be more pitiful,
  Even if the souls of serpents we had been."

As out of a green brand, that is on fire
  At one of the ends, and from the other drips
  And hisses with the wind that is escaping;

So from that splinter issued forth together
  Both words and blood; whereat I let the tip
  Fall, and stood like a man who is afraid.

"Had he been able sooner to believe,"
  My Sage made answer, "O thou wounded soul,
  What only in my verses he has seen,

Not upon thee had he stretched forth his hand;
  Whereas the thing incredible has caused me
  To put him to an act which grieveth me.

But tell him who thou wast, so that by way
  Of some amends thy fame he may refresh
  Up in the world, to which he can return."

And the trunk said: "So thy sweet words allure me,
  I cannot silent be; and you be vexed not,
  That I a little to discourse am tempted.

I am the one who both keys had in keeping
  Of Frederick's heart, and turned them to and fro
  So softly in unlocking and in locking,

That from his secrets most men I withheld;
  Fidelity I bore the glorious office
  So great, I lost thereby my sleep and pulses.

The courtesan who never from the dwelling
  Of Caesar turned aside her strumpet eyes,
  Death universal and the vice of courts,

Inflamed against me all the other minds,
  And they, inflamed, did so inflame Augustus,
  That my glad honours turned to dismal mournings.

My spirit, in disdainful exultation,
  Thinking by dying to escape disdain,
  Made me unjust against myself, the just.

I, by the roots unwonted of this wood,
  Do swear to you that never broke I faith
  Unto my lord, who was so worthy of honour;

And to the world if one of you return,
　Let him my memory comfort, which is lying
　Still prostrate from the blow that envy dealt it."

Waited awhile, and then: "Since he is silent,"
　The Poet said to me, "lose not the time,
　But speak, and question him, if more may please thee."

Whence I to him: "Do thou again inquire
　Concerning what thou thinks't will satisfy me;
　For I cannot, such pity is in my heart."

Therefore he recommenced: "So may the man
　Do for thee freely what thy speech implores,
　Spirit incarcerate, again be pleased

To tell us in what way the soul is bound
　Within these knots; and tell us, if thou canst,
　If any from such members e'er is freed."

Then blew the trunk amain, and afterward
　The wind was into such a voice converted:
　"With brevity shall be replied to you.

When the exasperated soul abandons
　The body whence it rent itself away,
　Minos consigns it to the seventh abyss.

It falls into the forest, and no part
　Is chosen for it; but where Fortune hurls it,
　There like a grain of spelt it germinates.

It springs a sapling, and a forest tree;
　The Harpies, feeding then upon its leaves,
　Do pain create, and for the pain an outlet.

Like others for our spoils shall we return;
　But not that any one may them revest,
　For 'tis not just to have what one casts off.

Here we shall drag them, and along the dismal
  Forest our bodies shall suspended be,
  Each to the thorn of his molested shade."

We were attentive still unto the trunk,
  Thinking that more it yet might wish to tell us,
  When by a tumult we were overtaken,

In the same way as he is who perceives
  The boar and chase approaching to his stand,
  Who hears the crashing of the beasts and branches;

And two behold! Upon our left-hand side,
  Naked and scratched, fleeing so furiously,
  That of the forest, every fan they broke.

He who was in advance: "Now help, Death, help!"
  And the other one, who seemed to lag too much,
  Was shouting: "Lano, were not so alert

Those legs of thine at joustings of the Toppo!"
  And then, perchance because his breath was failing,
  He grouped himself together with a bush.

Behind them was the forest full of black
  She-mastiffs, ravenous, and swift of foot
  As greyhounds, who are issuing from the chain.

On him who had crouched down they set their teeth,
  And him they lacerated piece by piece,
  Thereafter bore away those aching members.

Thereat my Escort took me by the hand,
  And led me to the bush, that all in vain
  Was weeping from its bloody lacerations.

"O Jacopo," it said, "of Sant' Andrea,
  What helped it thee of me to make a screen?
  What blame have I in thy nefarious life?"

When near him had the Master stayed his steps,
  He said: "Who wast thou, that through wounds so many
  Art blowing out with blood thy dolorous speech?"

And he to us: "O souls, that hither come
  To look upon the shameful massacre
  That has so rent away from me my leaves,

Gather them up beneath the dismal bush;
  I of that city was which to the Baptist
  Changed its first patron, wherefore he for this

Forever with his art will make it sad.
  And were it not that on the pass of Arno
  Some glimpses of him are remaining still,

Those citizens, who afterwards rebuilt it
  Upon the ashes left by Attila,
  In vain had caused their labour to be done.

Of my own house I made myself a gibbet."

❧CANTO XIV

On the edge of the wood lies a desert of burning sand where
flames rain down constantly. The shadows here are forced to
adopt different positions according to their sins. Thus the poets
behold supine Blasphemers and crouching Usurers, while the
Sodomites are made to wander about aimlessly. Dante recognises
Capaneus who died cursing Jove. The poets reach a blood-
red rivulet which prompts Dante to ask about the origins of
Phlegethon. Virgil replies by relating the story of the Old Man of
Crete whose tears coursed down to form the four rivers of Hell.

Because the charity of my native place
  Constrained me, gathered I the scattered leaves,
  And gave them back to him, who now was hoarse.

Then came we to the confine, where disparted
  The second round is from the third, and where
  A horrible form of Justice is beheld.

Clearly to manifest these novel things,
  I say that we arrived upon a plain,
  Which from its bed rejecteth every plant;

The dolorous forest is a garland to it
  All round about, as the sad moat to that;
  There close upon the edge we stayed our feet.

The soil was of an arid and thick sand,
  Not of another fashion made than that
  Which by the feet of Cato once was pressed.

Vengeance of God, O how much oughtest thou
  By each one to be dreaded, who doth read
  That which was manifest unto mine eyes!

Of naked souls beheld I many herds,
  Who all were weeping very miserably,
  And over them seemed set a law diverse.

Supine upon the ground some folk were lying;
  And some were sitting all drawn up together,
  And others went about continually.

Those who were going round were far the more,
  And those were less who lay down to their torment,
  But had their tongues more loosed to lamentation.

O'er all the sand-waste, with a gradual fall,
  Were raining down dilated flakes of fire,
  As of the snow on Alp without a wind.

As Alexander, in those torrid parts
  Of India, beheld upon his host
  Flames fall unbroken till they reached the ground.

Whence he provided with his phalanxes
  To trample down the soil, because the vapour
  Better extinguished was while it was single;

Thus was descending the eternal heat,
  Whereby the sand was set on fire, like tinder
  Beneath the steel, for doubling of the dole.

Without repose forever was the dance
  Of miserable hands, now there, now here,
  Shaking away from off them the fresh gleeds.

"Master," began I, "thou who overcomest
  All things except the demons dire, that issued
  Against us at the entrance of the gate,

Who is that mighty one who seems to heed not
  The fire, and lieth lowering and disdainful,
  So that the rain seems not to ripen him?"

And he himself, who had become aware
  That I was questioning my Guide about him,
  Cried: "Such as I was living, am I, dead.

If Jove should weary out his smith, from whom
  He seized in anger the sharp thunderbolt,
  Wherewith upon the last day I was smitten,

And if he wearied out by turns the others
  In Mongibello at the swarthy forge,
  Vociferating, 'Help, good Vulcan, help!'

Even as he did there at the fight of Phlegra,
  And shot his bolts at me with all his might,
  He would not have thereby a joyous vengeance."

Then did my Leader speak with such great force,
  That I had never heard him speak so loud:
  "O Capaneus, in that is not extinguished

Thine arrogance, thou punished art the more;
  Not any torment, saving thine own rage,
  Would be unto thy fury pain complete."

Then he turned round to me with better lip,
  Saying: "One of the Seven Kings was he
  Who Thebes besieged, and held, and seems to hold

God in disdain, and little seems to prize him;
  But, as I said to him, his own despites
  Are for his breast the fittest ornaments.

Now follow me, and mind thou do not place
  As yet thy feet upon the burning sand,
  But always keep them close unto the wood."

Speaking no word, we came to where there gushes
  Forth from the wood a little rivulet,
  Whose redness makes my hair still stand on end.

As from the Bulicame springs the brooklet,
  The sinful women later share among them,
  So downward through the sand it went its way.

The bottom of it, and both sloping banks,
  Were made of stone, and the margins at the side;
  Whence I perceived that there the passage was.

"In all the rest which I have shown to thee
  Since we have entered in within the gate
  Whose threshold unto no one is denied,

Nothing has been discovered by thine eyes
  So notable as is the present river,
  Which all the little flames above it quenches."

These words were of my Leader; whence I prayed him
  That he would give me largess of the food,
  For which he had given me largess of desire.

"In the mid-sea there sits a wasted land,"
  Said he thereafterward, "whose name is Crete,
  Under whose king the world of old was chaste.

There is a mountain there, that once was glad
  With waters and with leaves, which was called Ida;
  Now 'tis deserted, as a thing worn out.

Rhea once chose it for the faithful cradle
  Of her own son; and to conceal him better,
  Whene'er he cried, she there had clamours made.

A grand old man stands in the mount erect,
  Who holds his shoulders turned tow'rds Damietta,
  And looks at Rome as if it were his mirror.

His head is fashioned of refined gold,
  And of pure silver are the arms and breast;
  Then he is brass as far down as the fork.

From that point downward all is chosen iron,
  Save that the right foot is of kiln-baked clay,
  And more he stands on that than on the other.

Each part, except the gold, is by a fissure
  Asunder cleft, that dripping is with tears,
  Which gathered together perforate that cavern.

From rock to rock they fall into this valley;
  Acheron, Styx and Phlegethon they form;
  Then downward go along this narrow sluice

Unto that point where is no more descending.
  They form Cocytus; what that pool may be
  Thou shalt behold, so here 'tis not narrated."

And I to him: "If so the present runnel
  Doth take its rise in this way from our world,
  Why only on this verge appears it to us?"

And he to me: "Thou knowest the place is round,
  And notwithstanding thou hast journeyed far,
  Still to the left descending to the bottom,

Thou hast not yet through all the circle turned.
  Therefore if something new appear to us,
  It should not bring amazement to thy face."

And I again: "Master, where shall be found
  Lethe and Phlegethon, for of one thou'rt silent,
  And sayest the other of this rain is made?"

"In all thy questions truly thou dost please me,"
  Replied he; "but the boiling of the red
  Water might well solve one of them thou makest.

Thou shalt see Lethe, but outside this moat,
  There where the souls repair to lave themselves,
  When sin repented of has been removed."

Then said he: "It is time now to abandon
  The wood; take heed that thou come after me;
  A way the margins make that are not burning,

And over them all vapours are extinguished."

CANTO XV

*Virgil and Dante leave the burning plain by following
the channel through which the Phlegethon unwinds. A
company of Sodomites races towards them. One, Brunetto
Latini, Guelf statesman, writer and Dante's former
teacher, slows down. Brunetto prophesies that both political
parties in Florence will turn against Dante. His words
echo those of Ciacco in Canto VI. A cloud of smoke in the
distance announces the arrival of an alien group so the
Florentine sprints off to catch up with his companions.*

Now bears us onward one of the hard margins,
  And so the brooklet's mist o'ershadows it,
  From fire it saves the water and the dikes.

Even as the Flemings, 'twixt Cadsand and Bruges,
  Fearing the flood that tow'rds them hurls itself,
  Their bulwarks build to put the sea to flight;

And as the Paduans along the Brenta,
  To guard their villas and their villages,
  Or ever Chiarentana feel the heat;

In such similitude had those been made,
  Albeit not so lofty nor so thick,
  Whoever he might be, the master made them.

Now were we from the forest so remote,
  I could not have discovered where it was,
  Even if backward I had turned myself,

When we a company of souls encountered,
  Who came beside the dike, and every one
  Gazed at us, as at evening we are wont

To eye each other under a new moon,
  And so towards us sharpened they their brows
  As an old tailor at the needle's eye.

Thus scrutinised by such a family,
  By some one I was recognised, who seized
  My garment's hem, and cried out, "What a marvel!"

And I, when he stretched forth his arm to me,
  On his baked aspect fastened so mine eyes,
  That the scorched countenance prevented not

His recognition by my intellect;
  And bowing down my face unto his own,
  I made reply, "Are you here, Ser Brunetto?"

And he: "May't not displease thee, O my son,
  If a brief space with thee Brunetto Latini
  Backward return and let the trail go on."

I said to him: "With all my power I ask it;
  And if you wish me to sit down with you,
  I will, if he please, for I go with him."

"O son," he said, "whoever of this herd
  A moment stops, lies then a hundred years,
  Nor fans himself when smiteth him the fire.

Therefore go on; I at thy skirts will come,
  And afterward will I rejoin my band,
  Which goes lamenting its eternal doom."

I did not dare to go down from the road
  Level to walk with him; but my head bowed
  I held as one who goeth reverently.

And he began: "What fortune or what fate
  Before the last day leadeth thee down here?
  And who is this that showeth thee the way?"

"Up there above us in the life serene,"
  I answered him, "I lost me in a valley,
  Or ever yet my age had been completed.

But yestermorn I turned my back upon it;
  This one appeared to me, returning thither,
  And homeward leadeth me along this road."

And he to me: "If thou thy star do follow,
  Thou canst not fail thee of a glorious port,
  If well I judged in the life beautiful.

And if I had not died so prematurely,
  Seeing Heaven thus benignant unto thee,
  I would have given thee comfort in the work.

But that ungrateful and malignant people,
  Which of old time from Fesole descended,
  And smacks still of the mountain and the granite,

Will make itself, for thy good deeds, thy foe;
  And it is right; for among crabbed sorbs
  It ill befits the sweet fig to bear fruit.

Old rumour in the world proclaims them blind;
  A people avaricious, envious, proud;
  Take heed that of their customs thou do cleanse thee.

Thy fortune so much honour doth reserve thee,
  One party and the other shall be hungry
  For thee; but far from goat shall be the grass.

Their litter let the beasts of Fesole
  Make of themselves, nor let them touch the plant,
  If any still upon their dunghill rise,

In which may yet revive the consecrated
  Seed of those Romans, who remained there when
  The nest of such great malice it became."

"If my entreaty wholly were fulfilled,"
  Replied I to him, "not yet would you be
  In banishment from human nature placed;

For in my mind is fixed, and touches now
  My heart the dear and good paternal image
  Of you, when in the world from hour to hour

You taught me how a man becomes eternal;
  And how much I am grateful, while I live
  Behoves that in my language be discerned.

What you narrate of my career I write,
  And keep it to be glossed with other text
  By a Lady who can do it, if I reach her.

This much will I have manifest to you;
  Provided that my conscience do not chide me,
  For whatsoever Fortune I am ready.

Such handsel is not new unto mine ears;
  Therefore let Fortune turn her wheel around
  As it may please her, and the churl his mattock."

My Master thereupon on his right cheek
  Did backward turn himself, and looked at me;
  Then said: "He listeneth well who noteth it."

Nor speaking less on that account, I go
  With Ser Brunetto, and I ask who are
  His most known and most eminent companions.

And he to me: "To know of some is well;
  Of others it were laudable to be silent,
  For short would be the time for so much speech.

Know them in sum, that all of them were clerks,
  And men of letters great and of great fame,
  In the world tainted with the selfsame sin.

Priscian goes yonder with that wretched crowd,
  And Francis of Accorso; and thou hadst seen there
  If thou hadst had a hankering for such scurf,

That one, who by the Servant of the Servants
  From Arno was transferred to Bacchiglione,
  Where he has left his sin-excited nerves.

More would I say, but coming and discoursing
  Can be no longer; for that I behold
  New smoke uprising yonder from the sand.

A people comes with whom I may not be;
  Commended unto thee be my Tesoro,
  In which I still live, and no more I ask."

Then he turned round, and seemed to be of those
  Who at Verona run for the Green Mantle
  Across the plain; and seemed to be among them

The one who wins, and not the one who loses.

≈CANTO XVI

Still in the Circle of Violence, Dante hears the roar of a distant waterfall. Having recognized a fellow Florentine, three warrior Sodomites edge forward, all the while moving around him in a circle like a turning wheel. Their spokesman introduces himself as Jacopo Rusticucci and his two compatriots as Guido Guerra and Tegghiaio Aldobrand, both Guelf party leaders. These illustrious citizens of Florence ask for news of their city before moving away. The rush of the water is now deafening. Virgil removes the cord from around Dante's waist and throws it into the abyss. Some creature stirs below before swimming upwards.

Now was I where was heard the reverberation
  Of water falling into the next round,
  Like to that humming which the beehives make,

When shadows three together started forth,
  Running, from out a company that passed
  Beneath the rain of the sharp martyrdom.

Towards us came they, and each one cried out:
  "Stop, thou; for by thy garb to us thou seemest
  To be some one of our depraved city."

Ah me! What wounds I saw upon their limbs,
  Recent and ancient by the flames burnt in!
  It pains me still but to remember it.

Unto their cries my Teacher paused attentive;
  He turned his face towards me, and "Now wait,"
  He said; "to these we should be courteous.

And if it were not for the fire that darts
  The nature of this region, I should say
  That haste were more becoming thee than them."

As soon as we stood still, they recommenced
  The old refrain, and when they overtook us,
  Formed of themselves a wheel, all three of them.

As champions stripped and oiled are wont to do,
  Watching for their advantage and their hold,
  Before they come to blows and thrusts between them,

Thus, wheeling round, did every one his visage
  Direct to me, so that in opposite wise
  His neck and feet continual journey made.

And, "If the misery of this soft place
  Bring in disdain ourselves and our entreaties,"
  Began one, "and our aspect black and blistered,

Let the renown of us thy mind incline
  To tell us who thou art, who thus securely
  Thy living feet dost move along through Hell.

He in whose footprints thou dost see me treading,
  Naked and skinless though he now may go,
  Was of a greater rank than thou dost think;

He was the grandson of the good Gualdrada;
  His name was Guido Guerra, and in life
  Much did he with his wisdom and his sword.

The other, who close by me treads the sand,
  Tegghiaio Aldobrandi is, whose fame
  Above there in the world should welcome be.

And I, who with them on the cross am placed,
  Jacopo Rusticucci was; and truly
  My savage wife, more than aught else, doth harm me."

Could I have been protected from the fire,
  Below I should have thrown myself among them,
  And think the Teacher would have suffered it;

But as I should have burned and baked myself,
  My terror overmastered my good will,
  Which made me greedy of embracing them.

Then I began: "Sorrow and not disdain
  Did your condition fix within me so,
  That tardily it wholly is stripped off,

As soon as this my Lord said unto me
  Words, on account of which I thought within me
  That people such as you are were approaching.

I of your city am; and evermore
  Your labours and your honourable names
  I with affection have retraced and heard.

I leave the gall, and go for the sweet fruits
  Promised to me by the veracious Leader;
  But to the centre first I needs must plunge."

"So may the soul for a long while conduct
  Those limbs of thine," did he make answer then,
  "And so may thy renown shine after thee,

Valour and courtesy, say if they dwell
  Within our city, as they used to do,
  Or if they wholly have gone out of it;

For Guglielmo Borsier, who is in torment
  With us of late, and goes there with his comrades,
  Doth greatly mortify us with his words."

"The new inhabitants and the sudden gains,
  Pride and extravagance have in thee engendered,
  Florence, so that thou weep'st thereat already!"

In this wise I exclaimed with face uplifted;
  And the three, taking that for my reply,
  Looked at each other, as one looks at truth.

"If other times so little it doth cost thee",
  Replied they all, "to satisfy another,
  Happy art thou, thus speaking at thy will!

Therefore, if thou escape from these dark places,
  And come to rebehold the beauteous stars,
  When it shall pleasure thee to say, 'I was,'

See that thou speak of us unto the people."
  Then they broke up the wheel, and in their flight
  It seemed as if their agile legs were wings.

Not an Amen could possibly be said
  So rapidly as they had disappeared;
  Wherefore the Master deemed best to depart.

I followed him, and little had we gone,
  Before the sound of water was so near us,
  That speaking we should hardly have been heard.

Even as that stream which holdeth its own course
  The first from Monte Veso tow'rds the East,
  Upon the left-hand slope of Apennine,

Which is above called Acquacheta, ere
  It down descendeth into its low bed,
  And at Forli is vacant of that name,

Reverberates there above San Benedetto
  From Alps, by falling at a single leap,
  Where for a thousand there were room enough;

Thus downward from a bank precipitate,
  We found resounding that dark-tinted water,
  So that it soon the ear would have offended.

I had a cord around about me girt,
  And therewithal I whilom had designed
  To take the panther with the painted skin.

After I this had all from me unloosed,
  As my Conductor had commanded me,
  I reached it to him, gathered up and coiled,

Whereat he turned himself to the right side,
  And at a little distance from the verge,
  He cast it down into that deep abyss.

"It must needs be some novelty respond",
  I said within myself, "to the new signal
  The Master with his eye is following so."

Ah me! How very cautious men should be
  With those who not alone behold the act,
  But with their wisdom look into the thoughts!

He said to me: "Soon there will upward come
  What I await; and what thy thought is dreaming
  Must soon reveal itself unto thy sight."

Aye to that truth which has the face of falsehood,
  A man should close his lips as far as may be,
  Because without his fault it causes shame;

But here I cannot; and, Reader, by the notes
  Of this my Comedy to thee I swear,
  So may they not be void of lasting favour,

Athwart that dense and darksome atmosphere
  I saw a figure swimming upward come,
  Marvellous unto every steadfast heart,

Even as he returns who goeth down
  Sometimes to clear an anchor, which has grappled
  Reef, or aught else that in the sea is hidden,

Who upward stretches, and draws in his feet.

☙CANTO XVII

*Geryon appears as a monstrous personification of Fraud.
He has the head of an honest-looking man attached to
a snake-like body with a scorpion's sting at its end. The
Usurers, those who profited from lending money to others
at very high interest, are sitting on the edge of the abyss with
crested money pouches dangling from their necks. Dante
recognizes members of the eminent Gianfigliazzi, Ubriachi
and Scrovegni families. Virgil and Dante mount Geryon who
descends the Eighth Circle.*

"Behold the monster with the pointed tail,
  Who cleaves the hills, and breaketh walls and weapons,
  Behold him who infecteth all the world."

Thus unto me my Guide began to say,
  And beckoned him that he should come to shore,
  Near to the confine of the trodden marble;

And that uncleanly image of deceit
  Came up and thrust ashore its head and bust,
  But on the border did not drag its tail.

The face was as the face of a just man,
  Its semblance outwardly was so benign,
  And of a serpent all the trunk beside.

Two paws it had, hairy unto the armpits;
  The back, and breast, and both the sides it had
  Depicted o'er with nooses and with shields.

With colours more, groundwork or broidery
  Never in cloth did Tartars make nor Turks,
  Nor were such tissues by Arachne laid.

As sometimes wherries lie upon the shore,
  That part are in the water, part on land;
  And as among the guzzling Germans there,

The beaver plants himself to wage his war;
  So that vile monster lay upon the border,
  Which is of stone, and shutteth in the sand.

His tail was wholly quivering in the void,
  Contorting upwards the envenomed fork,
  That in the guise of scorpion armed its point.

The Guide said: "Now perforce must turn aside
  Our way a little, even to that beast
  Malevolent, that yonder coucheth him."

We therefore on the right side descended,
  And made ten steps upon the outer verge,
  Completely to avoid the sand and flame;

And after we are come to him, I see
  A little farther off upon the sand
  A people sitting near the hollow place.

Then said to me the Master: "So that full
  Experience of this round thou bear away,
  Now go and see what their condition is.

There let thy conversation be concise;
  Till thou returnest I will speak with him,
  That he concede to us his stalwart shoulders."

Thus farther still upon the outermost
  Head of that seventh circle all alone
  I went, where sat the melancholy folk.

Out of their eyes was gushing forth their woe;
  This way, that way, they helped them with their hands
  Now from the flames and now from the hot soil.

Not otherwise in summer do the dogs,
  Now with the foot, now with the muzzle, when
  By fleas, or flies, or gadflies, they are bitten.

When I had turned mine eyes upon the faces
  Of some, on whom the dolorous fire is falling,
  Not one of them I knew; but I perceived

That from the neck of each there hung a pouch,
  Which certain colour had, and certain blazon;
  And thereupon it seems their eyes are feeding.

And as I gazing round me come among them,
  Upon a yellow pouch I azure saw
  That had the face and posture of a lion.

Proceeding then the current of my sight,
  Another of them saw I, red as blood,
  Display a goose more white than butter is.

And one, who with an azure sow and gravid
  Emblazoned had his little pouch of white,
  Said unto me: "What dost thou in this moat?

Now get thee gone; and since thou'rt still alive,
  Know that a neighbour of mine, Vitaliano,
  Will have his seat here on my left-hand side.

A Paduan am I with these Florentines;
  Full many a time they thunder in mine ears,
  Exclaiming, 'Come the sovereign cavalier,

He who shall bring the satchel with three goats;'"
  Then twisted he his mouth, and forth he thrust
  His tongue, like to an ox that licks its nose.

And fearing lest my longer stay might vex
  Him who had warned me not to tarry long,
  Backward I turned me from those weary souls.

I found my Guide, who had already mounted
  Upon the back of that wild animal,
  And said to me: "Now be both strong and bold.

Now we descend by stairways such as these;
  Mount thou in front, for I will be midway,
  So that the tail may have no power to harm thee."

Such as he is who has so near the ague
  Of quartan that his nails are blue already,
  And trembles all, but looking at the shade;

Even such became I at those proffered words;
  But shame in me his menaces produced,
  Which maketh servant strong before good master.

I seated me upon those monstrous shoulders;
  I wished to say, and yet the voice came not
  As I believed, "Take heed that thou embrace me."

But he, who other times had rescued me
  In other peril, soon as I had mounted,
  Within his arms encircled and sustained me,

And said: "Now, Geryon, bestir thyself;
  The circles large, and the descent be little;
  Think of the novel burden which thou hast."

Even as the little vessel shoves from shore,
  Backward, still backward, so he thence withdrew;
  And when he wholly felt himself afloat,

There where his breast had been he turned his tail,
  And that extended like an eel he moved,
  And with his paws drew to himself the air.

A greater fear I do not think there was
  What time abandoned Phaeton the reins,
  Whereby the heavens, as still appears, were scorched;

Nor when the wretched Icarus his flanks
  Felt stripped of feathers by the melting wax,
  His father crying, "An ill way thou takest!"

Than was my own, when I perceived myself
  On all sides in the air, and saw extinguished
  The sight of everything but of the monster.

Onward he goeth, swimming slowly, slowly;
  Wheels and descends, but I perceive it only
  By wind upon my face and from below.

I heard already on the right the whirlpool
  Making a horrible crashing under us;
  Whence I thrust out my head with eyes cast downward.

Then was I still more fearful of the abyss;
  Because I fires beheld, and heard laments,
  Whereat I, trembling, all the closer cling.

I saw then, for before I had not seen it,
  The turning and descending, by great horrors
  That were approaching upon divers sides.

As falcon who has long been on the wing,
  Who, without seeing either lure or bird,
  Maketh the falconer say, "Ah me, thou stoopest,"

Descendeth weary, whence he started swiftly,
  Thorough a hundred circles, and alights
  Far from his master, sullen and disdainful;

Even thus did Geryon place us on the bottom,
  Close to the bases of the rough-hewn rock,
  And being disencumbered of our persons,

He sped away as arrow from the string.

CANTO XVIII

As the poets descend on Geryon's back in a slow gyre,
Dante describes his bird's-eye view of Hell's Eighth Circle
(malebolge). It has ten rocky clefts (bolgias), each one
connected to the next by a curved bridge. At the edge of the
first bolgia, two lines of naked souls are moving in opposite
directions – the Panders walking towards Virgil and Dante
and the Seducers filing past alongside them. Dante recognizes
Venedico Caccianemico, a Bolognese Guelf leader, and Jason
of the Argonauts. The second bolgia is characterized by the
foul stench of Flatterers drowning in excrement.

There is a place in Hell called Malebolge,
  Wholly of stone and of an iron colour,
  As is the circle that around it turns.

Right in the middle of the field malign
  There yawns a well exceeding wide and deep,
  Of which its place the structure will recount.

Round, then, is that enclosure which remains
  Between the well and foot of the high, hard bank,
  And has distinct in valleys ten its bottom.

As where for the protection of the walls
  Many and many moats surround the castles,
  The part in which they are a figure forms,

Just such an image those presented there;
  And as about such strongholds from their gates
  Unto the outer bank are little bridges,

So from the precipice's base did crags
  Project, which intersected dikes and moats,
  Unto the well that truncates and collects them.

Within this place, down shaken from the back
  Of Geryon, we found us; and the Poet
  Held to the left, and I moved on behind.

Upon my right hand I beheld new anguish,
  New torments, and new wielders of the lash,
  Wherewith the foremost *Bolgia* was replete.

Down at the bottom were the sinners naked;
  This side the middle came they facing us,
  Beyond it, with us, but with greater steps;

Even as the Romans, for the mighty host,
  The year of Jubilee, upon the bridge,
  Have chosen a mode to pass the people over;

For all upon one side towards the Castle
  Their faces have, and go unto St Peter's;
  On the other side they go towards the Mountain.

This side and that, along the livid stone
  Beheld I horned demons with great scourges,
  Who cruelly were beating them behind.

Ah me! How they did make them lift their legs
  At the first blows! And sooth not any one
  The second waited for, nor for the third.

While I was going on, mine eyes by one
  Encountered were; and straight I said: "Already
  With sight of this one I am not unfed."

Therefore I stayed my feet to make him out,
  And with me the sweet Guide came to a stand,
  And to my going somewhat back assented;

And he, the scourged one, thought to hide himself,
  Lowering his face, but little it availed him;
  For said I: "Thou that castest down thine eyes,

If false are not the features which thou bearest,
  Thou art Venedico Caccianimico;
  But what doth bring thee to such pungent sauces?"

And he to me: "Unwillingly I tell it;
  But forces me thine utterance distinct,
  Which makes me recollect the ancient world.

I was the one who the fair Ghisola
  Induced to grant the wishes of the Marquis,
  Howe'er the shameless story may be told.

Not the sole Bolognese am I who weeps here;
  Nay, rather is this place so full of them,
  That not so many tongues today are taught

'Twixt Reno and Savena to say 'sipa';
  And if thereof thou wishest pledge or proof,
  Bring to thy mind our avaricious heart."

While speaking in this manner, with his scourge
  A demon smote him, and said: "Get thee gone
  Pander, there are no women here for coin."

I joined myself again unto mine Escort;
  Thereafterward with footsteps few we came
  To where a crag projected from the bank.

This very easily did we ascend,
  And turning to the right along its ridge,
  From those eternal circles we departed.

When we were there, where it is hollowed out
  Beneath, to give a passage to the scourged,
  The Guide said: "Wait, and see that on thee strike

The vision of those others evil-born,
  Of whom thou hast not yet beheld the faces,
  Because together with us they have gone."

From the old bridge we looked upon the train
  Which tow'rds us came upon the other border,
  And which the scourges in like manner smite.

And the good Master, without my inquiring,
  Said to me: "See that tall one who is coming,
  And for his pain seems not to shed a tear;

Still what a royal aspect he retains!
  That Jason is, who by his heart and cunning
  The Colchians of the Ram made destitute.

He by the isle of Lemnos passed along
  After the daring women pitiless
  Had unto death devoted all their males.

There with his tokens and with ornate words
  Did he deceive Hypsipyle, the maiden
  Who first, herself, had all the rest deceived.

There did he leave her pregnant and forlorn;
  Such sin unto such punishment condemns him,
  And also for Medea is vengeance done.

With him go those who in such wise deceive;
  And this sufficient be of the first valley
  To know, and those that in its jaws it holds."

We were already where the narrow path
  Crosses athwart the second dike, and forms
  Of that a buttress for another arch.

Thence we heard people, who are making moan
  In the next *Bolgia*, snorting with their muzzles,
  And with their palms beating upon themselves

The margins were incrusted with a mould
  By exhalation from below, that sticks there,
  And with the eyes and nostrils wages war.

The bottom is so deep, no place suffices
  To give us sight of it, without ascending
  The arch's back, where most the crag impends.

Thither we came, and thence down in the moat
  I saw a people smothered in a filth
  That out of human privies seemed to flow;

And whilst below there with mine eye I search,
  I saw one with his head so foul with ordure,
  It was not clear if he were clerk or layman.

He screamed to me: "Wherefore art thou so eager
  To look at me more than the other foul ones?"
  And I to him: "Because, if I remember,

I have already seen thee with dry hair,
  And thou'rt Alessio Interminei of Lucca;
  Therefore I eye thee more than all the others."

And he thereon, belabouring his pumpkin:
  "The flatteries have submerged me here below,
  Wherewith my tongue was never surfeited."

Then said to me the Guide: "See that thou thrust
  Thy visage somewhat farther in advance,
  That with thine eyes thou well the face attain

Of that uncleanly and dishevelled drab,
  Who there doth scratch herself with filthy nails,
  And crouches now, and now on foot is standing.

Thais the harlot is it, who replied
  Unto her paramour, when he said, 'Have I
  Great gratitude from thee?' – 'Nay, marvellous;'

And herewith let our sight be satisfied."

☙CANTO XIX

Crossing the bridge into the third bolgia, *Virgil and Dante enter a landscape full of holes from which protrude the flaming, flailing legs of the Simonists. In life, these fraudulent ecclesiastics profited from the Church and its offices. Dante questions a pair of legs and discovers they belong to Pope Nicholas III, who mistakes him for Boniface VIII, the next pope destined to fall down that hole. According to the Simonist's eloquent prophecy, Pope Clement V is third in line. Dante expresses his moral indignation in equally ornate language. Virgil rewards his progress by carrying him to the arch above the fourth* bolgia.

O Simon Magus, O forlorn disciples,
  Ye who the things of God, which ought to be
  The brides of holiness, rapaciously

For silver and for gold do prostitute,
  Now it behoves for you the trumpet sound,
  Because in this third *Bolgia* ye abide.

We had already on the following tomb
  Ascended to that portion of the crag
  Which o'er the middle of the moat hangs plumb.

Wisdom supreme, O how great art thou showest
  In heaven, in Earth, and in the evil world,
  And with what justice doth thy power distribute!

I saw upon the sides and on the bottom
  The livid stone with perforations filled,
  All of one size, and every one was round.

To me less ample seemed they not, nor greater
  Than those that in my beautiful Saint John
  Are fashioned for the place of the baptisers,

And one of which, not many years ago,
　　I broke for some one, who was drowning in it;
　　Be this a seal all men to undeceive.

Out of the mouth of each one there protruded
　　The feet of a transgressor, and the legs
　　Up to the calf, the rest within remained.

In all of them the soles were both on fire;
　　Wherefore the joints so violently quivered,
　　They would have snapped asunder withes and bands.

Even as the flame of unctuous things is wont
　　To move upon the outer surface only,
　　So likewise was it there from heel to point.

"Master, who is that one who writhes himself,
　　More than his other comrades quivering,"
　　I said, "and whom a redder flame is sucking?"

And he to me: "If thou wilt have me bear thee
　　Down there along that bank which lowest lies,
　　From him thou'lt know his errors and himself."

And I: "What pleases thee, to me is pleasing;
　　Thou art my Lord, and knowest that I depart not
　　From thy desire, and knowest what is not spoken."

Straightway upon the fourth dike we arrived;
　　We turned, and on the left-hand side descended
　　Down to the bottom full of holes and narrow.

And the good Master yet from off his haunch
　　Deposed me not, till to the hole he brought me
　　Of him who so lamented with his shanks.

"Whoe'er thou art, that standest upside down,
　　O doleful soul, implanted like a stake,"
　　To say began I, "if thou canst, speak out."

I stood even as the friar who is confessing
  The false assassin, who, when he is fixed,
  Recalls him, so that death may be delayed.

And he cried out: "Dost thou stand there already,
  Dost thou stand there already, Boniface?
  By many years the record lied to me.

Art thou so early satiate with that wealth,
  For which thou didst not fear to take by fraud
  The beautiful Lady, and then work her woe?"

Such I became, as people are who stand,
  Not comprehending what is answered them,
  As if bemocked, and know not how to answer.

Then said Virgilius: "Say to him straightway,
  'I am not he, I am not he thou thinkest.'"
  And I replied as was imposed on me.

Whereat the spirit writhed with both his feet,
  Then, sighing, with a voice of lamentation
  Said to me: "Then what wantest thou of me?

If who I am thou carest so much to know,
  That thou on that account hast crossed the bank,
  Know that I vested was with the great mantle;

And truly was I son of the She-bear,
  So eager to advance the cubs, that wealth
  Above, and here myself, I pocketed.

Beneath my head the others are dragged down
  Who have preceded me in simony,
  Flattened along the fissure of the rock.

Below there I shall likewise fall, whenever
  That one shall come who I believed thou wast,
  What time the sudden question I proposed.

But longer I my feet already toast,
  And here have been in this way upside down,
  Than he will planted stay with reddened feet;

For after him shall come of fouler deed
  From tow'rds the west a Pastor without law,
  Such as befits to cover him and me.

New Jason will he be, of whom we read
  In Maccabees; and as his king was pliant,
  So he who governs France shall be to this one."

I do not know if I were here too bold,
  That him I answered only in this metre:
  "I pray thee tell me now how great a treasure

Our Lord demanded of Saint Peter first,
  Before he put the keys into his keeping?
  Truly he nothing asked but 'Follow me'.

Nor Peter nor the rest asked of Matthias
  Silver or gold, when he by lot was chosen
  Unto the place the guilty soul had lost.

Therefore stay here, for thou art justly punished,
  And keep safe guard o'er the ill-gotten money,
  Which caused thee to be valiant against Charles.

And were it not that still forbids it me
  The reverence for the keys superlative
  Thou hadst in keeping in the gladsome life,

I would make use of words more grievous still;
  Because your avarice afflicts the world,
  Trampling the good and lifting the depraved.

The Evangelist you Pastors had in mind,
  When she who sitteth upon many waters
  To fornicate with kings by him was seen;

The same who with the seven heads was born,
  And power and strength from the ten horns received,
  So long as virtue to her spouse was pleasing.

Ye have made yourselves a god of gold and silver;
  And from the idolater how differ ye,
  Save that he one, and ye a hundred worship?

Ah, Constantine! Of how much ill was mother,
  Not thy conversion, but that marriage dower
  Which the first wealthy Father took from thee!"

And while I sang to him such notes as these,
  Either that anger or that conscience stung him,
  He struggled violently with both his feet.

I think in sooth that it my Leader pleased,
  With such contented lip he listened ever
  Unto the sound of the true words expressed.

Therefore with both his arms he took me up,
  And when he had me all upon his breast,
  Remounted by the way where he descended.

Nor did he tire to have me clasped to him;
  But bore me to the summit of the arch
  Which from the fourth dike to the fifth is passage.

There tenderly he laid his burden down,
  Tenderly on the crag uneven and steep,
  That would have been hard passage for the goats:

Thence was unveiled to me another valley.

✑CANTO XX

The Soothsayers or Sorcerers, a group of weeping shadows, mournfully make their way along the valley of the fourth bolgia. On Earth, they claimed they could look into the future but, in the afterlife, their heads are twisted around so completely that their tears fall on their buttocks. Virgil recognizes Amphiaraus, Tiresias, Aruns and Manto (the last one a former citizen of his Mantuan birthplace). After discussing the founding of the city, he names more of the damned.

Of a new pain behoves me to make verses
  And give material to the twentieth canto
  Of the first song, which is of the submerged.

I was already thoroughly disposed
  To peer down into the uncovered depth,
  Which bathed itself with tears of agony;

And people saw I through the circular valley,
  Silent and weeping, coming at the pace
  Which in this world the Litanies assume.

As lower down my sight descended on them,
  Wondrously each one seemed to be distorted
  From chin to the beginning of the chest;

For tow'rds the reins the countenance was turned,
  And backward it behoved them to advance,
  As to look forward had been taken from them.

Perchance indeed by violence of palsy
  Some one has been thus wholly turned awry;
  But I ne'er saw it, nor believe it can be.

As God may let thee, Reader, gather fruit
  From this thy reading, think now for thyself
  How I could ever keep my face unmoistened,

When our own image near me I beheld
  Distorted so, the weeping of the eyes
  Along the fissure bathed the hinder parts.

Truly I wept, leaning upon a peak
  Of the hard crag, so that my Escort said
  To me: "Art thou, too, of the other fools?

Here pity lives when it is wholly dead;
  Who is a greater reprobate than he
  Who feels compassion at the doom divine?

Lift up, lift up thy head, and see for whom
  Opened the earth before the Thebans' eyes;
  Wherefore they all cried: 'Whither rushest thou,

Amphiaraus? Why dost leave the war?'
  And downward ceased he not to fall amain
  As far as Minos, who lays hold on all.

See, he has made a bosom of his shoulders!
  Because he wished to see too far before him
  Behind he looks, and backward goes his way:

Behold Tiresias, who his semblance changed,
  When from a male a female he became,
  His members being all of them transformed;

And afterwards was forced to strike once more
  The two entangled serpents with his rod,
  Ere he could have again his manly plumes.

That Aruns is, who backs the other's belly,
  Who in the hills of Luni, there where grubs
  The Carrarese who houses underneath,

Among the marbles white a cavern had
  For his abode; whence to behold the stars
  And sea, the view was not cut off from him.

And she there, who is covering up her breasts,
  Which thou beholdest not, with loosened tresses,
  And on that side has all the hairy skin,

Was Manto, who made quest through many lands,
  Afterwards tarried there where I was born;
  Whereof I would thou list to me a little.

After her father had from life departed,
  And the city of Bacchus had become enslaved,
  She a long season wandered through the world.

Above in beauteous Italy lies a lake
  At the Alp's foot that shuts in Germany
  Over Tyrol, and has the name Benaco.

By a thousand springs, I think, and more, is bathed,
  'Twixt Garda and Val Camonica, Pennino,
  With water that grows stagnant in that lake.

Midway a place is where the Trentine Pastor,
  And he of Brescia, and the Veronese
  Might give his blessing, if he passed that way.

Sitteth Peschiera, fortress fair and strong,
  To front the Brescians and the Bergamasks,
  Where round about the bank descendeth lowest.

There of necessity must fall whatever
  In bosom of Benaco cannot stay,
  And grows a river down through verdant pastures.

Soon as the water doth begin to run,
  No more Benaco is it called, but Mincio,
  Far as Governo, where it falls in Po.

Not far it runs before it finds a plain
  In which it spreads itself, and makes it marshy,
  And oft 'tis wont in summer to be sickly.

Passing that way the virgin pitiless
  Land in the middle of the fen descried,
  Untilled and naked of inhabitants;

There to escape all human intercourse,
  She with her servants stayed, her arts to practise
  And lived, and left her empty body there.

The men, thereafter, who were scattered round,
  Collected in that place, which was made strong
  By the lagoon it had on every side;

They built their city over those dead bones,
  And, after her who first the place selected,
  Mantua named it, without other omen.

Its people once within more crowded were,
  Ere the stupidity of Casalodi
  From Pinamonte had received deceit.

Therefore I caution thee, if e'er thou hearest
  Originate my city otherwise,
  No falsehood may the verity defraud."

And I: "My Master, thy discourses are
  To me so certain, and so take my faith,
  That unto me the rest would be spent coals.

But tell me of the people who are passing,
  If any one note-worthy thou beholdest,
  For only unto that my mind reverts."

Then said he to me: "He who from the cheek
  Thrusts out his beard upon his swarthy shoulders
  Was, at the time when Greece was void of males,

So that there scarce remained one in the cradle,
  An augur, and with Calchas gave the moment,
  In Aulis, when to sever the first cable.

Eryphylus his name was, and so sings
  My lofty Tragedy in some part or other;
  That knowest thou well, who knowest the whole of it.

The next, who is so slender in the flanks,
  Was Michael Scott, who of a verity
  Of magical illusions knew the game.

Behold Guido Bonatti, behold Asdente,
  Who now unto his leather and his thread
  Would fain have stuck, but he too late repents.

Behold the wretched ones, who left the needle,
  The spool and rock, and made them fortune-tellers;
  They wrought their magic spells with herb and
      image.

But come now, for already holds the confines
  Of both the hemispheres, and under Seville
  Touches the ocean-wave, Cain and the thorns,

And yesternight the moon was round already;
  Thou shouldst remember well it did not harm thee
  From time to time within the forest deep."

Thus spake he to me, and we walked the while.

☙CANTO XXI

*Virgil and Dante stand on the arch that spans the fifth
bolgia. They see black devils running along it, with sinners
over their shoulders which they cast into a ditch bubbling
with pitch. These are Barrators, who sinned against the
State and are now tormented by a company of pitchfork-
wielding Malebranche devils. Dante hides while Virgil
addresses their captain, Malacoda, declaring that Heaven
wills him and another to pass. The devils exchange obscene
parting salutes as a team of them escorts the poets to a
different bridge (the sixth one lies broken).*

From bridge to bridge thus, speaking other things
  Of which my Comedy cares not to sing,
  We came along, and held the summit, when

We halted to behold another fissure
  Of Malebolge and other vain laments;
  And I beheld it marvellously dark.

As in the Arsenal of the Venetians
  Boils in the winter the tenacious pitch
  To smear their unsound vessels o'er again,

For sail they cannot; and instead thereof
  One makes his vessel new, and one recaulks
  The ribs of that which many a voyage has made;

One hammers at the prow, one at the stern,
  This one makes oars, and that one cordage twists,
  Another mends the mainsail and the mizzen;

Thus, not by fire, but by the art divine,
  Was boiling down below there a dense pitch
  Which upon every side the bank belimed.

I saw it, but I did not see within it
  Aught but the bubbles that the boiling raised,
  And all swell up and resubside compressed.

The while below there fixedly I gazed,
  My Leader, crying out: "Beware, beware!"
  Drew me unto himself from where I stood.

Then I turned round, as one who is impatient
  To see what it behoves him to escape,
  And whom a sudden terror doth unman,

Who, while he looks, delays not his departure;
  And I beheld behind us a black devil,
  Running along upon the crag, approach.

Ah, how ferocious was he in his aspect!
  And how he seemed to me in action ruthless,
  With open wings and light upon his feet!

His shoulders, which sharp-pointed were and high,
  A sinner did encumber with both haunches,
  And he held clutched the sinews of the feet.

From off our bridge, he said: "O Malebranche,
  Behold one of the elders of Saint Zita;
  Plunge him beneath, for I return for others

Unto that town, which is well furnished with them.
  All there are barrators, except Bonturo;
  No into Yes for money there is changed."

He hurled him down, and over the hard crag
  Turned round, and never was a mastiff loosened
  In so much hurry to pursue a thief.

The other sank, and rose again face downward;
  But the demons, under cover of the bridge,
  Cried: "Here the Santo Volto has no place!

Here swims one otherwise than in the Serchio;
  Therefore, if for our gaffs thou wishest not,
  Do not uplift thyself above the pitch."

They seized him then with more than a hundred rakes;
  They said: "It here behoves thee to dance covered,
  That, if thou canst, thou secretly mayest pilfer."

Not otherwise the cooks their scullions make
  Immerse into the middle of the caldron
  The meat with hooks, so that it may not float.

Said the good Master to me: "That it be not
  Apparent thou art here, crouch thyself down
  Behind a jag, that thou mayest have some screen;

And for no outrage that is done to me
  Be thou afraid, because these things I know,
  For once before was I in such a scuffle."

Then he passed on beyond the bridge's head,
  And as upon the sixth bank he arrived,
  Need was for him to have a steadfast front.

With the same fury, and the same uproar,
  As dogs leap out upon a mendicant,
  Who on a sudden begs, where'er he stops,

They issued from beneath the little bridge,
  And turned against him all their grappling-irons;
  But he cried out: "Be none of you malignant!

Before those hooks of yours lay hold of me,
  Let one of you step forward, who may hear me,
  And then take counsel as to grappling me."

They all cried out: "Let Malacoda go;"
  Whereat one started, and the rest stood still,
  And he came to him, saying: "What avails it?"

"Thinkest thou, Malacoda, to behold me
  Advanced into this place," my Master said,
  "Safe hitherto from all your skill of fence,

Without the will divine, and fate auspicious?
  Let me go on, for it in Heaven is willed
  That I another show this savage road."

Then was his arrogance so humbled in him,
  That he let fall his grapnel at his feet,
  And to the others said: "Now strike him not."

And unto me my Guide: "O thou, who sittest
  Among the splinters of the bridge crouched down,
  Securely now return to me again."

Wherefore I started and came swiftly to him;
  And all the devils forward thrust themselves,
  So that I feared they would not keep their compact.

And thus beheld I once afraid the soldiers
  Who issued under safeguard from Caprona,
  Seeing themselves among so many foes.

Close did I press myself with all my person
  Beside my Leader, and turned not mine eyes
  From off their countenance, which was not good.

They lowered their rakes, and "Wilt thou have me hit him",
  They said to one another, "on the rump?"
  And answered: "Yes; see that thou nick him with it."

But the same demon who was holding parley
  With my Conductor turned him very quickly,
  And said: "Be quiet, be quiet, Scarmiglione;"

Then said to us: "You can no farther go
  Forward upon this crag, because is lying
  All shattered, at the bottom, the sixth arch.

And if it still doth please you to go onward,
  Pursue your way along upon this rock;
  Near is another crag that yields a path.

Yesterday, five hours later than this hour,
  One thousand and two hundred sixty-six
  Years were complete, that here the way was broken.

I send in that direction some of mine
  To see if any one doth air himself;
  Go ye with them; for they will not be vicious.

Step forward, Alichino and Calcabrina,"
  Began he to cry out, "and thou, Cagnazzo;
  And Barbariccia, do thou guide the ten.

Come forward, Libicocco and Draghignazzo,
  And tusked Ciriatto and Graffiacane,
  And Farfarello and mad Rubicante;

Search ye all round about the boiling pitch;
  Let these be safe as far as the next crag,
  That all unbroken passes o'er the dens."

"O me! What is it, Master, that I see?
  Pray let us go", I said, "without an escort,
  If thou knowest how, since for myself I ask none.

If thou art as observant as thy wont is,
  Dost thou not see that they do gnash their teeth,
  And with their brows are threatening woe to us?"

And he to me: "I will not have thee fear;
  Let them gnash on, according to their fancy,
  Because they do it for those boiling wretches."

Along the left-hand dike they wheeled about;
  But first had each one thrust his tongue between
  His teeth towards their leader for a signal;

And he had made a trumpet of his rump.

CANTO XXII

Dante compares Malacoda's salute to the kinds of military signals he knows. Any Barrators who are seen squatting in the pitch dive underneath the surface as soon as any devil comes near. A sinner from Navarre falls into the clutches of Graffiacan and is torn apart. Questioned by Virgil during these antics, the Navarrese sinner tricks the devils into momentarily looking away on the promise that he will lure others, like Friar Gomita and Michael Zanche, to the surface. As he plunges into the pitch and escapes, two devils rush in after him and have to be rescued by Barbarricia. A fight ensues.

I have erewhile seen horsemen moving camp,
  Begin the storming, and their muster make,
  And sometimes starting off for their escape;

Vaunt-couriers have I seen upon your land,
  O Aretines, and foragers go forth,
  Tournaments stricken, and the joustings run,

Sometimes with trumpets and sometimes with bells,
  With kettle-drums, and signals of the castles,
  And with our own, and with outlandish things,

But never yet with bagpipe so uncouth
  Did I see horsemen move, nor infantry,
  Nor ship by any sign of land or star.

We went upon our way with the ten demons;
  Ah, savage company! But in the church
  With saints, and in the tavern with the gluttons!

Ever upon the pitch was my intent,
  To see the whole condition of that *Bolgia*,
  And of the people who therein were burned.

Even as the dolphins, when they make a sign
  To mariners by arching of the back,
  That they should counsel take to save their vessel,

Thus sometimes, to alleviate his pain,
  One of the sinners would display his back,
  And in less time conceal it than it lightens.

As on the brink of water in a ditch
  The frogs stand only with their muzzles out,
  So that they hide their feet and other bulk,

So upon every side the sinners stood;
  But ever as Barbariccia near them came,
  Thus underneath the boiling they withdrew.

I saw, and still my heart doth shudder at it,
  One waiting thus, even as it comes to pass
  One frog remains, and down another dives;

And Graffiacan, who most confronted him,
  Grappled him by his tresses smeared with pitch,
  And drew him up, so that he seemed an otter.

I knew, before, the names of all of them,
  So had I noted them when they were chosen,
  And when they called each other, listened how.

"O Rubicante, see that thou do lay
  Thy claws upon him, so that thou mayst flay him,"
  Cried all together the accursed ones.

And I: "My Master, see to it, if thou canst,
  That thou mayst know who is the luckless wight,
  Thus come into his adversaries' hands."

Near to the side of him my Leader drew,
  Asked of him whence he was; and he replied:
  "I in the kingdom of Navarre was born;

My mother placed me servant to a lord,
  For she had borne me to a ribald knave,
  Destroyer of himself and of his things.

Then I domestic was of good King Thibault;
  I set me there to practise barratry,
  For which I pay the reckoning in this heat."

And Ciriatto, from whose mouth projected,
  On either side, a tusk, as in a boar,
  Caused him to feel how one of them could rip.

Among malicious cats the mouse had come;
  But Barbariccia clasped him in his arms,
  And said: "Stand ye aside, while I enfork him."

And to my Master he turned round his head;
  "Ask him again," he said, "if more thou wish
  To know from him, before someone destroy him."

The Guide: "Now tell then of the other culprits;
  Knowest thou any one who is a Latian,
  Under the pitch?" And he: "I separated

Lately from one who was a neighbour to it;
  Would that I still were covered up with him,
  For I should fear not either claw nor hook!"

And Libicocco: "We have borne too much;"
  And with his grapnel seized him by the arm,
  So that, by rending, he tore off a tendon.

Eke Draghignazzo wished to pounce upon him
  Down at the legs; whence their Decurion
  Turned round and round about with evil look.

When they again somewhat were pacified,
  Of him, who still was looking at his wound,
  Demanded my Conductor without stay:

"Who was that one, from whom a luckless parting
　　Thou sayest thou hast made, to come ashore?"
　　And he replied: "It was the Friar Gomita,

He of Gallura, vessel of all fraud,
　　Who had the enemies of his Lord in hand,
　　And dealt so with them each exults thereat;

Money he took, and let them smoothly off,
　　As he says; and in other offices
　　A barrator was he, not mean but sovereign.

Foregathers with him one Don Michael Zanche
　　Of Logodoro; and of Sardinia
　　To gossip never do their tongues feel tired.

O me! See that one, how he grinds his teeth;
　　Still farther would I speak, but am afraid
　　Lest he to scratch my itch be making ready."

And the grand Provost, turned to Farfarello,
　　Who rolled his eyes about as if to strike,
　　Said: "Stand aside there, thou malicious bird."

"If you desire either to see or hear,"
　　The terror-stricken recommenced thereon,
　　"Tuscans or Lombards, I will make them come.

But let the Malebranche cease a little,
　　So that these may not their revenges fear,
　　And I, down sitting in this very place,

For one that I am will make seven come,
　　When I shall whistle, as our custom is
　　To do whenever one of us comes out."

Cagnazzo at these words his muzzle lifted,
　　Shaking his head, and said: "Just hear the trick
　　Which he has thought of, down to throw himself!"

Whence he, who snares in great abundance had,
  Responded: "I by far too cunning am,
  When I procure for mine a greater sadness."

Alichin held not in, but running counter
  Unto the rest, said to him: "If thou dive,
  I will not follow thee upon the gallop,

But I will beat my wings above the pitch;
  The height be left, and be the bank a shield
  To see if thou alone dost countervail us."

O thou who readest, thou shalt hear new sport!
  Each to the other side his eyes averted;
  He first, who most reluctant was to do it.

The Navarrese selected well his time;
  Planted his feet on land, and in a moment
  Leaped, and released himself from their design.

Whereat each one was suddenly stung with shame,
  But he most who was cause of the defeat;
  Therefore he moved, and cried: "Thou art o'ertaken."

But little it availed, for wings could not
  Outstrip the fear; the other one went under,
  And, flying, upward he his breast directed;

Not otherwise the duck upon a sudden
  Dives under, when the falcon is approaching,
  And upward he returneth cross and weary.

Infuriate at the mockery, Calcabrina
  Flying behind him followed close, desirous
  The other should escape, to have a quarrel.

And when the barrator had disappeared,
  He turned his talons upon his companion,
  And grappled with him right above the moat.

But sooth the other was a doughty sparhawk
  To clapperclaw him well; and both of them
  Fell in the middle of the boiling pond.

A sudden intercessor was the heat;
  But ne'ertheless of rising there was naught,
  To such degree they had their wings belimed.

Lamenting with the others, Barbariccia
  Made four of them fly to the other side
  With all their gaffs, and very speedily

This side and that they to their posts descended;
  They stretched their hooks towards the pitch-ensnared,
  Who were already baked within the crust,

And in this manner busied did we leave them.

⤞CANTO XXIII

The sinner's skirmish with the devils reminds Dante of the
frog, mouse and hawk fable, where each animal successively
deceives the other. Sensing danger, Virgil grabs Dante
and they run to the edge of the ravine and slide down into
the sixth bolgia. *Looking up, they see the devils and are*
thankful for their escape. The weeping Hypocrites approach
in single file, wearing gilded but heavy, lead-lined cloaks.
The worst hypocrite of all, Caiaphas, Pontius Pilate's evil
counsellor, stands crucified and impaled by three stakes.
Virgil is angry to discover that Malacoda lied about
the bridge in Canto XXI – they will have to climb up a
rockslide instead.

Silent, alone, and without company
  We went, the one in front, the other after,
  As go the Minor Friars along their way.

Upon the fable of Aesop was directed
  My thought, by reason of the present quarrel,
  Where he has spoken of the frog and mouse;

For *mo* and *issa* are not more alike
  Than this one is to that, if well we couple
  End and beginning with a steadfast mind.

And even as one thought from another springs,
  So afterward from that was born another,
  Which the first fear within me double made.

Thus did I ponder: "These on our account
  Are laughed to scorn, with injury and scoff
  So great, that much I think it must annoy them.

If anger be engrafted on ill-will,
  They will come after us more merciless
  Than dog upon the leveret which he seizes,"

I felt my hair stand all on end already
  With terror, and stood backwardly intent,
  When said I: "Master, if thou hidest not

Thyself and me forthwith, of Malebranche
  I am in dread; we have them now behind us;
  I so imagine them, I already feel them."

And he: "If I were made of leaded glass,
  Thine outward image I should not attract
  Sooner to me than I imprint the inner.

Just now thy thoughts came in among my own,
  With similar attitude and similar face,
  So that of both one counsel sole I made.

If peradventure the right bank so slope
  That we to the next *Bolgia* can descend,
  We shall escape from the imagined chase."

Not yet he finished rendering such opinion,
  When I beheld them come with outstretched wings,
  Not far remote, with will to seize upon us.

My Leader on a sudden seized me up,
  Even as a mother who by noise is wakened,
  And close beside her sees the enkindled flames,

Who takes her son, and flies, and does not stop,
  Having more care of him than of herself,
  So that she clothes her only with a shift;

And downward from the top of the hard bank
  Supine he gave him to the pendent rock,
  That one side of the other *Bolgia* walls.

Ne'er ran so swiftly water through a sluice
  To turn the wheel of any land-built mill,
  When nearest to the paddles it approaches,

As did my Master down along that border,
  Bearing me with him on his breast away,
  As his own son, and not as a companion.

Hardly the bed of the ravine below
  His feet had reached, ere they had reached the hill
  Right over us; but he was not afraid;

For the high Providence, which had ordained
  To place them ministers of the fifth moat,
  The power of thence departing took from all.

A painted people there below we found,
  Who went about with footsteps very slow,
  Weeping and in their semblance tired and vanquished.

They had on mantles with the hoods low down
  Before their eyes, and fashioned of the cut
  That in Cologne they for the monks are made.

Without, they gilded are so that it dazzles;
  But inwardly all leaden and so heavy
  That Frederick used to put them on of straw.

O everlastingly fatiguing mantle!
  Again we turned us, still to the left hand
  Along with them, intent on their sad plaint;

But owing to the weight, that weary folk
  Came on so tardily, that we were new
  In company at each motion of the haunch.

Whence I unto my Leader: "See thou find
  Some one who may by deed or name be known,
  And thus in going move thine eye about."

And one, who understood the Tuscan speech,
  Cried to us from behind: "Stay ye your feet,
  Ye, who so run athwart the dusky air!

Perhaps thou'lt have from me what thou demandest."
  Whereat the Leader turned him, and said: "Wait,
  And then according to his pace proceed."

I stopped, and two beheld I show great haste
  Of spirit, in their faces, to be with me;
  But the burden and the narrow way delayed them.

When they came up, long with an eye askance
  They scanned me without uttering a word.
  Then to each other turned, and said together:

"He by the action of his throat seems living;
  And if they dead are, by what privilege
  Go they uncovered by the heavy stole?"

Then said to me: "Tuscan, who to the college
  Of miserable hypocrites art come,
  Do not disdain to tell us who thou art."

And I to them: "Born was I, and grew up
  In the great town on the fair river of Arno,
  And with the body am I've always had.

But who are ye, in whom there trickles down
  Along your cheeks such grief as I behold?
  And what pain is upon you, that so sparkles?"

And one replied to me: "These orange cloaks
  Are made of lead so heavy, that the weights
  Cause in this way their balances to creak.

Frati Gaudenti were we, and Bolognese;
  I Catalano, and he Loderingo
  Named, and together taken by thy city,

As the wont is to take one man alone,
  For maintenance of its peace; and we were such
  That still it is apparent round Gardingo."

"O Friars," began I, "your iniquitous. . ."
  But said no more; for to mine eyes there rushed
  One crucified with three stakes on the ground.

When me he saw, he writhed himself all over,
  Blowing into his beard with suspirations;
  And the Friar Catalan, who noticed this,

Said to me: "This transfixed one, whom thou seest,
  Counselled the Pharisees that it was meet
  To put one man to torture for the people.

Crosswise and naked is he on the path,
  As thou perceivest; and he needs must feel,
  Whoever passes, first how much he weighs;

And in like mode his father-in-law is punished
  Within this moat, and the others of the council,
  Which for the Jews was a malignant seed."

And thereupon I saw Virgilius marvel
  O'er him who was extended on the cross
  So vilely in eternal banishment.

Then he directed to the Friar this voice:
  "Be not displeased, if granted thee, to tell us
  If to the right hand any pass slope down

By which we two may issue forth from here,
  Without constraining some of the black angels
  To come and extricate us from this deep."

Then he made answer: "Nearer than thou hopest
  There is a rock, that forth from the great circle
  Proceeds, and crosses all the cruel valleys,

Save that at this 'tis broken, and does not bridge it;
  You will be able to mount up the ruin,
  That sidelong slopes and at the bottom rises."

The Leader stood awhile with head bowed down;
  Then said: "The business badly he recounted
  Who grapples with his hook the sinners yonder."

And the Friar: "Many of the Devil's vices
  Once heard I at Bologna, and among them,
  That he's a liar and the father of lies."

Thereat my Leader with great strides went on,
  Somewhat disturbed with anger in his looks;
  Whence from the heavy-laden I departed

After the prints of his beloved feet.

⤳CANTO XXIV

Teacher and pupil begin their arduous ascent of the fallen bridge. Crossing back into the seventh bolgia, *they hear sounds in the darkness. Once at the top, Dante cannot catch his breath. At the edge of the eighth* bolgia, *they behold a chaotic scene of running Thieves being attacked by serpents. One reptile darts out and strikes a blow to a sinner's neck. He catches fire and turns into a pile of ashes before being restored to his mortal form – that of Vanni Fucci, a sacristy thief from Pistoia. He, too, predicts political strife for Florence.*

In that part of the youthful year wherein
  The Sun his locks beneath Aquarius tempers,
  And now the nights draw near to half the day,

What time the hoar-frost copies on the ground
  The outward semblance of her sister white,
  But little lasts the temper of her pen,

The husbandman, whose forage faileth him,
  Rises, and looks, and seeth the champaign
  All gleaming white, whereat he beats his flank,

Returns in doors, and up and down laments,
  Like a poor wretch, who knows not what to do;
  Then he returns and hope revives again,

Seeing the world has changed its countenance
  In little time, and takes his shepherd's crook,
  And forth the little lambs to pasture drives.

Thus did the Master fill me with alarm,
  When I beheld his forehead so disturbed,
  And to the ailment came as soon the plaster.

For as we came unto the ruined bridge,
　　The Leader turned to me with that sweet look
　　Which at the mountain's foot I first beheld.

His arms he opened, after some advisement
　　Within himself elected, looking first
　　Well at the ruin, and laid hold of me.

And even as he who acts and meditates,
　　For aye it seems that he provides beforehand,
　　So upward lifting me towards the summit

Of a huge rock, he scanned another crag,
　　Saying: "To that one grapple afterwards,
　　But try first if 'tis such that it will hold thee."

This was no way for one clothed with a cloak;
　　For hardly we, he light, and I pushed upward,
　　Were able to ascend from jag to jag.

And had it not been, that upon that precinct
　　Shorter was the ascent than on the other,
　　He I know not, but I had been dead beat.

But because Malebolge tow'rds the mouth
　　Of the profoundest well is all inclining,
　　The structure of each valley doth import

That one bank rises and the other sinks.
　　Still we arrived at length upon the point
　　Wherefrom the last stone breaks itself asunder.

The breath was from my lungs so milked away,
　　When I was up, that I could go no farther,
　　Nay, I sat down upon my first arrival.

"Now it behoves thee thus to put off sloth,"
　　My Master said; "for sitting upon down,
　　Or under quilt, one cometh not to fame,

Withouten which whoso his life consumes
  Such vestige leaveth of himself on Earth,
  As smoke in air or in the water foam.

And therefore raise thee up, o'ercome the anguish
  With spirit that o'ercometh every battle,
  If with its heavy body it sink not.

A longer stairway it behoves thee mount;
  'Tis not enough from these to have departed;
  Let it avail thee, if thou understand me."

Then I uprose, showing myself provided
  Better with breath than I did feel myself,
  And said: "Go on, for I am strong and bold."

Upward we took our way along the crag,
  Which jagged was, and narrow, and difficult,
  And more precipitous far than that before.

Speaking I went, not to appear exhausted;
  Whereat a voice from the next moat came forth,
  Not well adapted to articulate words.

I know not what it said, though o'er the back
  I now was of the arch that passes there;
  But he seemed moved to anger who was speaking.

I was bent downward, but my living eyes
  Could not attain the bottom, for the dark;
  Wherefore I: "Master, see that thou arrive

At the next round, and let us descend the wall;
  For as from hence I hear and understand not,
  So I look down and nothing I distinguish."

"Other response", he said, "I make thee not,
  Except the doing; for the modest asking
  Ought to be followed by the deed in silence."

We from the bridge descended at its head,
  Where it connects itself with the eighth bank,
  And then was manifest to me the *Bolgia*;

And I beheld therein a terrible throng
  Of serpents, and of such a monstrous kind,
  That the remembrance still congeals my blood

Let Libya boast no longer with her sand;
  For if Chelydri, Jaculi and Phareae
  She breeds, with Cenchri and with Amphisbaena,

Neither so many plagues nor so malignant
  E'er showed she with all Ethiopia,
  Nor with whatever on the Red Sea is!

Among this cruel and most dismal throng
  People were running naked and affrighted.
  Without the hope of hole or heliotrope.

They had their hands with serpents bound behind them;
  These riveted upon their reins the tail
  And head, and were in front of them entwined.

And lo! At one who was upon our side
  There darted forth a serpent, which transfixed him
  There where the neck is knotted to the shoulders.

Nor "O" so quickly e'er, nor "I" was written,
  As he took fire, and burned; and ashes wholly
  Behoved it that in falling he became.

And when he on the ground was thus destroyed,
  The ashes drew together, and of themselves
  Into himself they instantly returned.

Even thus by the great sages 'tis confessed
  The phoenix dies, and then is born again,
  When it approaches its five-hundredth year;

On herb or grain it feeds not in its life,
  But only on tears of incense and amomum,
  And nard and myrrh are its last winding-sheet.

And as he is who falls, and knows not how,
  By force of demons who to earth down drag him,
  Or other oppilation that binds man,

When he arises and around him looks,
  Wholly bewildered by the mighty anguish
  Which he has suffered, and in looking sighs;

Such was that sinner after he had risen.
  Justice of God! O how severe it is,
  That blows like these in vengeance poureth down!

The Guide thereafter asked him who he was;
  Whence he replied: "I rained from Tuscany
  A short time since into this cruel gorge.

A bestial life, and not a human, pleased me,
  Even as the mule I was; I'm Vanni Fucci,
  Beast, and Pistoia was my worthy den."

And I unto the Guide: "Tell him to stir not,
  And ask what crime has thrust him here below,
  For once a man of blood and wrath I saw him."

And the sinner, who had heard, dissembled not,
  But unto me directed mind and face,
  And with a melancholy shame was painted.

Then said: "It pains me more that thou hast caught me
  Amid this misery where thou seest me,
  Than when I from the other life was taken.

What thou demandest I cannot deny;
  So low am I put down because I robbed
  The sacristy of the fair ornaments,

And falsely once 'twas laid upon another;
  But that thou mayst not such a sight enjoy,
  If thou shalt e'er be out of the dark places,

Thine ears to my announcement ope and hear:
  Pistoia first of Neri groweth meagre;
  Then Florence doth renew her men and manners;

Mars draws a vapour up from Val di Magra,
  Which is with turbid clouds enveloped round,
  And with impetuous and bitter tempest

Over Campo Picen shall be the battle;
  When it shall suddenly rend the mist asunder,
  So that each Bianco shall thereby be smitten.

And this I've said that it may give thee pain."

☙CANTO XXV

Vanni Fucci, the militant leader from Pistoia, makes an
obscene gesture towards God with his fist before being
immobilized by a bevy of snakes who wrap themselves around
him. When he breaks free, Cacus the Centaur gallops off in
pursuit, with a fire-belching dragon on his shoulders. Three
shadows appear. They are looking for Cianfa, who appears
as a man-become-snake. He attacks Agnello, with whom he
merges into one monstrous being. Another shadow exchanges
his serpentine form with Buoso. Only Puccio Sciancato
retains his shape.

At the conclusion of his words, the thief
  Lifted his hands aloft with both the figs,
  Crying: "Take that, God, for at thee I aim them."

From that time forth the serpents were my friends;
  For one entwined itself about his neck
  As if it said: "I will not thou speak more;"

And round his arms another, and rebound him,
  Clinching itself together so in front,
  That with them he could not a motion make.

Pistoia, ah, Pistoia! Why resolve not
  To burn thyself to ashes and so perish,
  Since in ill-doing thou thy seed excellest?

Through all the sombre circles of this Hell,
  Spirit I saw not against God so proud,
  Not he who fell at Thebes down from the walls!

He fled away, and spake no further word;
  And I beheld a Centaur full of rage
  Come crying out: "Where is, where is the scoffer?"

I do not think Maremma has so many
  Serpents as he had all along his back,
  As far as where our countenance begins.

Upon the shoulders, just behind the nape,
  With wings wide open was a dragon lying,
  And he sets fire to all that he encounters.

My Master said: "That one is Cacus, who
  Beneath the rock upon Mount Aventine
  Created oftentimes a lake of blood.

He goes not on the same road with his brothers,
  By reason of the fraudulent theft he made
  Of the great herd, which he had near to him;

Whereat his tortuous actions ceased beneath
  The mace of Hercules, who peradventure
  Gave him a hundred, and he felt not ten."

While he was speaking thus, he had passed by,
  And spirits three had underneath us come,
  Of which nor I aware was, nor my Leader,

Until what time they shouted: "Who are you?"
  On which account our story made a halt,
  And then we were intent on them alone.

I did not know them; but it came to pass,
  As it is wont to happen by some chance,
  That one to name the other was compelled,

Exclaiming: "Where can Cianfa have remained?"
  Whence I, so that the Leader might attend,
  Upward from chin to nose my finger laid.

If thou art, Reader, slow now to believe
  What I shall say, it will no marvel be,
  For I who saw it hardly can admit it.

As I was holding raised on them my brows,
  Behold! A serpent with six feet darts forth
  In front of one, and fastens wholly on him.

With middle feet it bound him round the paunch,
  And with the forward ones his arms it seized;
  Then thrust its teeth through one cheek and the other;

The hindermost it stretched upon his thighs,
  And put its tail through in between the two,
  And up behind along the reins outspread it.

Ivy was never fastened by its barbs
  Unto a tree so, as this horrible reptile
  Upon the other's limbs entwined its own.

Then they stuck close, as if of heated wax
  They had been made, and intermixed their colour;
  Nor one nor other seemed now what he was;

E'en as proceedeth on before the flame
  Upward along the paper a brown colour,
  Which is not black as yet, and the white dies.

The other two looked on, and each of them
  Cried out: "O me, Agnello, how thou changest!
  Behold, thou now art neither two nor one."

Already the two heads had one become,
  When there appeared to us two figures mingled
  Into one face, wherein the two were lost.

Of the four lists were fashioned the two arms,
  The thighs and legs, the belly and the chest
  Members became that never yet were seen.

Every original aspect there was cancelled;
  Two and yet none did the perverted image
  Appear, and such departed with slow pace.

Even as a lizard, under the great scourge
　Of days canicular, exchanging hedge,
　Lightning appeareth if the road it cross;

Thus did appear, coming towards the bellies
　Of the two others, a small fiery serpent,
　Livid and black as is a peppercorn.

And in that part whereat is first received
　Our aliment, it one of them transfixed;
　Then downward fell in front of him extended.

The one transfixed looked at it, but said naught;
　Nay, rather with feet motionless he yawned,
　Just as if sleep or fever had assailed him.

He at the serpent gazed, and it at him;
　One through the wound, the other through the mouth
　Smoked violently, and the smoke commingled.

Henceforth be silent Lucan, where he mentions
　Wretched Sabellus and Nassidius,
　And wait to hear what now shall be shot forth.

Be silent Ovid, of Cadmus and Arethusa;
　For if him to a snake, her to fountain,
　Converts he fabling, that I grudge him not;

Because two natures never front to front
　Has he transmuted, so that both the forms
　To interchange their matter ready were.

Together they responded in such wise,
　That to a fork the serpent cleft his tail,
　And eke the wounded drew his feet together.

The legs together with the thighs themselves
　Adhered so, that in little time the juncture
　No sign whatever made that was apparent.

He with the cloven tail assumed the figure
  The other one was losing, and his skin
  Became elastic, and the other's hard.

I saw the arms draw inward at the armpits,
  And both feet of the reptile, that were short,
  Lengthen as much as those contracted were.

Thereafter the hind feet, together twisted,
  Became the member that a man conceals,
  And of his own the wretch had two created.

While both of them the exhalation veils
  With a new colour, and engenders hair
  On one of them and depilates the other,

The one uprose and down the other fell,
  Though turning not away their impious lamps,
  Underneath which each one his muzzle changed.

He who was standing drew it tow'rds the temples,
  And from excess of matter, which came thither,
  Issued the ears from out the hollow cheeks;

What did not backward run and was retained
  Of that excess made to the face a nose,
  And the lips thickened far as was befitting.

He who lay prostrate thrusts his muzzle forward,
  And backward draws the ears into his head,
  In the same manner as the snail its horns;

And so the tongue, which was entire and apt
  For speech before, is cleft, and the bi-forked
  In the other closes up, and the smoke ceases.

The soul, which to a reptile had been changed,
  Along the valley hissing takes to flight,
  And after him the other speaking sputters.

Then did he turn upon him his new shoulders,
  And said to the other: "I'll have Buoso run,
  Crawling as I have done, along this road."

In this way I beheld the seventh ballast
  Shift and reshift, and here be my excuse
  The novelty, if aught my pen transgress.

And notwithstanding that mine eyes might be
  Somewhat bewildered, and my mind dismayed,
  They could not flee away so secretly

But that I plainly saw Puccio Sciancato;
  And he it was who sole of three companions,
  Which came in the beginning, was not changed;

The other was he whom thou, Gaville, weepest.

❧CANTO XXVI

The rocky rise above the eighth bolgia *is characterized by flickering flames, each of which contains the soul of a Deceiver. One of the flames, curiously split in two, catches Dante's attention. He is told that it houses a pair of Trojan warriors, Ulysses and Diomed, who are being jointly punished for fraudulent counselling. Virgil interrogates the pair for Dante's benefit. Ulysses recalls his final voyage, on which he sailed past the Pillars of Hercules (Strait of Gibraltar) and into the forbidden sea (Atlantic Ocean), where a whirlwind rose up and spun his vessel around before sinking it.*

Rejoice, O Florence, since thou art so great,
  That over sea and land thou beatest thy wings,
  And throughout Hell thy name is spread abroad!

Among the thieves five citizens of thine
  Like these I found, whence shame comes unto me,
  And thou thereby to no great honour risest.

But if when morn is near our dreams are true,
  Feel shalt thou in a little time from now
  What Prato, if none other, craves for thee.

And if it now were, it were not too soon;
  Would that it were, seeing it needs must be,
  For 'twill aggrieve me more the more I age.

We went our way, and up along the stairs
  The bourns had made us to descend before,
  Remounted my Conductor and drew me.

And following the solitary path
  Among the rocks and ridges of the crag,
  The foot without the hand sped not at all.

Then sorrowed I, and sorrow now again,
  When I direct my mind to what I saw,
  And more my genius curb than I am wont,

That it may run not unless virtue guide it;
  So that if some good star, or better thing,
  Have given me good, I may myself not grudge it.

As many as the hind (who on the hill
  Rests at the time when he who lights the world
  His countenance keeps least concealed from us,

While as the fly gives place unto the gnat)
  Seeth the glow-worms down along the valley,
  Perchance there where he ploughs and makes his vintage;

With flames as manifold resplendent all
  Was the eighth *Bolgia*, as I grew aware
  As soon as I was where the depth appeared.

And such as he who with the bears avenged him
  Beheld Elijah's chariot at departing,
  What time the steeds to heaven erect uprose,

For with his eye he could not follow it
  So as to see aught else than flame alone,
  Even as a little cloud ascending upward,

Thus each along the gorge of the intrenchment
  Was moving; for not one reveals the theft,
  And every flame a sinner steals away.

I stood upon the bridge uprisen to see,
  So that, if I had seized not on a rock,
  Down had I fallen without being pushed.

And the Leader, who beheld me so attent,
  Exclaimed: "Within the fires the spirits are;
  Each swathes himself with that wherewith he burns."

"My Master," I replied, "by hearing thee
  I am more sure; but I surmised already
  It might be so, and already wished to ask thee

Who is within that fire, which comes so cleft
  At top, it seems uprising from the pyre
  Where was Eteocles with his brother placed."

He answered me: "Within there are tormented
  Ulysses and Diomed, and thus together
  They unto vengeance run as unto wrath.

And there within their flame do they lament
  The ambush of the horse, which made the door
  Whence issued forth the Romans' gentle seed;

Therein is wept the craft, for which being dead
  Deidamia still deplores Achilles,
  And pain for the Palladium there is borne."

"If they within those sparks possess the power
  To speak," I said, "thee, Master, much I pray,
  And re-pray, that the prayer be worth a thousand,

That thou make no denial of awaiting
  Until the horned flame shall hither come;
  Thou seest that with desire I lean towards it."

And he to me: "Worthy is thy entreaty
  Of much applause, and therefore I accept it;
  But take heed that thy tongue restrain itself.

Leave me to speak, because I have conceived
  That which thou wishest; for they might disdain
  Perchance, since they were Greeks, discourse of thine."

When now the flame had come unto that point,
  Where to my Leader it seemed time and place,
  After this fashion did I hear him speak:

"O ye, who are twofold within one fire,
  If I deserved of you, while I was living,
  If I deserved of you or much or little

When in the world I wrote the lofty verses,
  Do not move on, but one of you declare
  Whither, being lost, he went away to die."

Then of the antique flame the greater horn,
  Murmuring, began to wave itself about
  Even as a flame doth which the wind fatigues.

Thereafterward, the summit to and fro
  Moving as if it were the tongue that spake,
  It uttered forth a voice, and said: "When I

From Circe had departed, who concealed me
  More than a year there near unto Gaeta,
  Or ever yet Aeneas named it so,

Nor fondness for my son, nor reverence
  For my old father, nor the due affection
  Which joyous should have made Penelope,

Could overcome within me the desire
  I had to be experienced of the world,
  And of the vice and virtue of mankind;

But I put forth on the high open sea
  With one sole ship, and that small company
  By which I never had deserted been.

Both of the shores I saw as far as Spain,
  Far as Morocco, and the isle of Sardes,
  And the others which that sea bathes round about.

I and my company were old and slow
  When at that narrow passage we arrived
  Where Hercules his landmarks set as signals,

That man no farther onward should adventure.
  On the right hand behind me left I Seville,
  And on the other already had left Ceuta.

'O brothers, who amid a hundred thousand
  Perils', I said, 'have come unto the West,
  To this so inconsiderable vigil

Which is remaining of your senses still
  Be ye unwilling to deny the knowledge,
  Following the sun, of the unpeopled world.

Consider ye the seed from which ye sprang;
  Ye were not made to live like unto brutes,
  But for pursuit of virtue and of knowledge.'

So eager did I render my companions,
  With this brief exhortation, for the voyage,
  That then I hardly could have held them back.

And having turned our stern unto the morning,
  We of the oars made wings for our mad flight,
  Evermore gaining on the larboard side.

Already all the stars of the other pole
  The night beheld, and ours so very low
  It did not rise above the ocean floor.

Five times rekindled and as many quenched
  Had been the splendour underneath the moon,
  Since we had entered into the deep pass,

When there appeared to us a mountain, dim
  From distance, and it seemed to me so high
  As I had never any one beheld.

Joyful were we, and soon it turned to weeping;
  For out of the new land a whirlwind rose,
  And smote upon the fore part of the ship.

Three times it made her whirl with all the waters,
  At the fourth time it made the stern uplift,
  And the prow downward go, as pleased Another,

Until the sea above us closed again."

✎ CANTO XXVII

Another flame draws near, having recognized Virgil's
Lombard accent. It asks for tidings of its native region and
pleads that its identity and life story remain undisclosed
but it is none other than Guido Da Montefeltro. This
well-known deceiver joined the Franciscan order in old age
after a high-profile military career as a Ghibelline captain.
Breaking his vows, he adopted military fraud to guide Pope
Boniface VIII to victory against the Colonna family and
uttered a fraudulent repentance on his deathbed, trusting
in the pontificate's fake absolution.

Already was the flame erect and quiet,
  To speak no more, and now departed from us
  With the permission of the gentle Poet;

When yet another, which behind it came,
  Caused us to turn our eyes upon its top
  By a confused sound that issued from it.

As the Sicilian bull (that bellowed first
  With the lament of him, and that was right,
  Who with his file had modulated it)

Bellowed so with the voice of the afflicted,
  That, notwithstanding it was made of brass,
  Still it appeared with agony transfixed;

Thus, by not having any way or issue
  At first from out the fire, to its own language
  Converted were the melancholy words.

But afterwards, when they had gathered way
  Up through the point, giving it that vibration
  The tongue had given them in their passage out,

We heard it said: "O thou, at whom I aim
  My voice, and who but now wast speaking Lombard,
  Saying, 'Now go thy way, no more I urge thee,'

Because I come perchance a little late,
  To stay and speak with me let it not irk thee;
  Thou seest it irks not me, and I am burning.

If thou but lately into this blind world
  Hast fallen down from that sweet Latian land,
  Wherefrom I bring the whole of my transgression,

Say, if the Romagnuols have peace or war,
  For I was from the mountains there between
  Urbino and the yoke whence Tiber bursts."

I still was downward bent and listening,
  When my Conductor touched me on the side,
  Saying: "Speak thou: this one a Latian is."

And I, who had beforehand my reply
  In readiness, forthwith began to speak:
  "O soul, that down below there art concealed,

Romagna thine is not and never has been
  Without war in the bosom of its tyrants;
  But open war I none have left there now.

Ravenna stands as it long years has stood;
  The Eagle of Polenta there is brooding,
  So that she covers Cervia with her vans.

The city which once made the long resistance,
  And of the French a sanguinary heap,
  Beneath the Green Paws finds itself again;

Verrucchio's ancient Mastiff and the new,
  Who made such bad disposal of Montagna,
  Where they are wont make wimbles of their teeth.

The cities of Lamone and Santerno
  Governs the Lioncel of the white lair,
  Who changes sides 'twixt summer-time and winter;

And that of which the Savio bathes the flank,
  Even as it lies between the plain and mountain,
  Lives between tyranny and a free state.

Now I entreat thee tell us who thou art;
  Be not more stubborn than the rest have been,
  So may thy name hold front there in the world."

After the fire a little more had roared
  In its own fashion, the sharp point it moved
  This way and that, and then gave forth such breath:

"If I believed that my reply were made
  To one who to the world would e'er return,
  This flame without more flickering would stand still;

But inasmuch as never from this depth
  Did any one return, if I hear true,
  Without the fear of infamy I answer,

I was a man of arms, then Cordelier,
  Believing thus begirt to make amends;
  And truly my belief had been fulfilled

But for the High Priest, whom may ill betide,
  Who put me back into my former sins;
  And how and wherefore I will have thee hear.

While I was still the form of bone and pulp
  My mother gave to me, the deeds I did
  Were not those of a lion, but a fox.

The machinations and the covert ways
  I knew them all, and practised so their craft,
  That to the ends of Earth the sound went forth.

When now unto that portion of mine age
  I saw myself arrived, when each one ought
  To lower the sails, and coil away the ropes,

That which before had pleased me then displeased me;
  And penitent and confessing I surrendered,
  Ah woe is me! And it would have bestead me;

The Leader of the modern Pharisees
  Having a war near unto Lateran,
  And not with Saracens nor with the Jews,

For each one of his enemies was Christian,
  And none of them had been to conquer Acre,
  Nor merchandising in the Sultan's land,

Nor the high office, nor the sacred orders,
  In him regarded, nor in me that cord
  Which used to make those girt with it more meagre;

But even as Constantine sought out Sylvester
  To cure his leprosy, within Soracte,
  So this one sought me out as an adept

To cure him of the fever of his pride.
  Counsel he asked of me, and I was silent,
  Because his words appeared inebriate.

And then he said: 'Be not thy heart afraid;
  Henceforth I thee absolve; and thou instruct me
  How to raze Palestrina to the ground.

Heaven have I power to lock and to unlock,
  As thou dost know; therefore the keys are two,
  The which my predecessor held not dear.'

Then urged me on his weighty arguments
  There, where my silence was the worst advice;
  And said I: 'Father, since thou washest me

Of that sin into which I now must fall,
  The promise long with the fulfilment short
  Will make thee triumph in thy lofty seat.'

Francis came afterward, when I was dead,
  For me; but one of the black Cherubim
  Said to him: 'Take him not; do me no wrong;

He must come down among my servitors,
  Because he gave the fraudulent advice
  From which time forth I have been at his hair;

For who repents not cannot be absolved,
  Nor can one both repent and will at once,
  Because of the contradiction which consents not.'

O miserable me! How I did shudder
  When he seized on me, saying: 'Peradventure
  Thou didst not think that I was a logician!'

He bore me unto Minos, who entwined
  Eight times his tail about his stubborn back,
  And after he had bitten it in great rage,

Said: 'Of the thievish fire a culprit this;'
  Wherefore, here where thou seest, am I lost,
  And vested thus in going I bemoan me."

When it had thus completed its recital,
  The flame departed uttering lamentations,
  Writhing and flapping its sharp-pointed horn.

Onward we passed, both I and my Conductor,
  Up o'er the crag above another arch,
  Which the moat covers, where is paid the fee

By those who, sowing discord, win their burden.

❧CANTO XXVIII

In the ninth bolgia, *the large crowds of the Sowers of Discord are disfigured and dismembered, many with their intestines spilling out. Several instigators of scandal and schism are named, including the Prophet Mahomet, founder of Islam, split open from crotch to chin, and Ali, his son-in-law. The sinners curse their lot and stir Dante's pity before predicting the unsavoury end of certain Italians who are still alive. The image of the medieval French troubadour Bertram De Born carrying his decapitated head in his hand is a vivid example of Dantean divine retribution or contrapasso, where his wits are literally "separated" from his body.*

Who ever could, e'en with untrammelled words,
  Tell of the blood and of the wounds in full
  Which now I saw, by many times narrating?

Each tongue would for a certainty fall short
  By reason of our speech and memory,
  That have small room to comprehend so much.

If were again assembled all the people
  Which formerly upon the fateful land
  Of Puglia were lamenting for their blood

Shed by the Romans and the lingering war
  That of the rings made such illustrious spoils,
  As Livy has recorded, who errs not,

With those who felt the agony of blows
  By making counterstand to Robert Guiscard,
  And all the rest, whose bones are gathered still

At Ceperano, where a renegade
  Was each Apulian, and at Tagliacozzo,
  Where without arms the old Alardo conquered,

And one his limb transpierced, and one lopped off,
  Should show, it would be nothing to compare
  With the disgusting mode of the ninth *Bolgia*.

A cask by losing centre-piece or cant
  Was never shattered so, as I saw one
  Rent from the chin to where one breaketh wind.

Between his legs were hanging down his entrails;
  His heart was visible, and the dismal sack
  That maketh excrement of what is eaten.

While I was all absorbed in seeing him,
  He looked at me, and opened with his hands
  His bosom, saying: "See now how I rend me;

How mutilated, see, is Mahomet;
  In front of me doth Ali weeping go,
  Cleft in the face from forelock unto chin;

And all the others whom thou here beholdest,
  Disseminators of scandal and of schism
  While living were, and therefore are cleft thus.

A devil is behind here, who doth cleave us
  Thus cruelly, unto the falchion's edge
  Putting again each one of all this ream,

When we have gone around the doleful road;
  By reason that our wounds are closed again
  Ere any one in front of him repass.

But who art thou, that musest on the crag,
  Perchance to postpone going to the pain
  That is adjudged upon thine accusations?"

"Nor death hath reached him yet, nor guilt doth bring him",
  My Master made reply, "to be tormented;
  But to procure him full experience,

Me, who am dead, behoves it to conduct him
  Down here through Hell, from circle unto circle;
  And this is true as that I speak to thee."

More than a hundred were there when they heard him,
  Who in the moat stood still to look at me,
  Through wonderment oblivious of their torture.

"Now say to Fra Dolcino, then, to arm him,
  Thou, who perhaps wilt shortly see the sun,
  If soon he wish not here to follow me,

So with provisions, that no stress of snow
  May give the victory to the Novarese,
  Which otherwise to gain would not be easy."

After one foot to go away he lifted,
  This word did Mahomet say unto me,
  Then to depart upon the ground he stretched it.

Another one, who had his throat pierced through,
  And nose cut off close underneath the brows,
  And had no longer but a single ear,

Staying to look in wonder with the others,
  Before the others did his gullet open,
  Which outwardly was red in every part,

And said: "O thou, whom guilt doth not condemn,
  And whom I once saw up in Latian land,
  Unless too great similitude deceive me,

Call to remembrance Pier da Medicina,
  If e'er thou see again the lovely plain
  That from Vercelli slopes to Marcabo,

And make it known to the best two of Fano,
  To Messer Guido and Angiolello likewise,
  That if foreseeing here be not in vain,

Cast over from their vessel shall they be,
  And drowned near unto the Cattolica,
  By the betrayal of a tyrant fell.

Between the isles of Cyprus and Majorca
  Neptune ne'er yet beheld so great a crime,
  Neither of pirates nor Argolic people.

That traitor, who sees only with one eye,
  And holds the land, which some one here with me
  Would fain be fasting from the vision of,

Will make them come unto a parley with him;
  Then will do so, that to Focara's wind
  They will not stand in need of vow or prayer."

And I to him: "Show to me and declare,
  If thou wouldst have me bear up news of thee,
  Who is this person of the bitter vision."

Then did he lay his hand upon the jaw
  Of one of his companions, and his mouth
  Oped, crying: "This is he, and he speaks not.

This one, being banished, every doubt submerged
  In Caesar by affirming the forearmed
  Always with detriment allowed delay."

O how bewildered unto me appeared,
  With tongue asunder in his windpipe slit,
  Curio, who in speaking was so bold!

And one, who both his hands dissevered had,
  The stumps uplifting through the murky air,
  So that the blood made horrible his face,

Cried out: "Thou shalt remember Mosca also,
  Who said, alas! 'A thing done has an end!'
  Which was an ill seed for the Tuscan people."

"And death unto thy race," thereto I added;
  Whence he, accumulating woe on woe,
  Departed, like a person sad and crazed.

But I remained to look upon the crowd;
  And saw a thing which I should be afraid,
  Without some further proof, even to recount,

If it were not that conscience reassures me,
  That good companion which emboldens man
  Beneath the hauberk of its feeling pure.

I truly saw, and still I seem to see it,
  A trunk without a head walk in like manner
  As walked the others of the mournful herd.

And by the hair it held the head dissevered,
  Hung from the hand in fashion of a lantern,
  And that upon us gazed and said: "O me!"

It of itself made to itself a lamp,
  And they were two in one, and one in two;
  How that can be, He knows who so ordains it.

When it was come close to the bridge's foot,
  It lifted high its arm with all the head,
  To bring more closely unto us its words,

Which were: "Behold now the sore penalty,
  Thou, who dost breathing go the dead beholding;
  Behold if any be as great as this.

And so that thou may carry news of me,
  Know that Bertram de Born am I, the same
  Who gave to the Young King the evil comfort.

I made the father and the son rebellious;
  Achitophel not more with Absalom
  And David did with his accursed goadings.

Because I parted persons so united,
  Parted do I now bear my brain, alas!
  From its beginning, which is in this trunk.

Thus is observed in me the counterpoise."

CANTO XXIX

When Virgil chides his pupil for showering such prolonged attention upon these wretches, Dante argues that he is searching for someone in particular. Virgil swears having seen Geri del Bello, first cousin to Dante's father, pointing a finger at him. The pair continue their discussion of the sinner. In the tenth bolgia, *they find all kinds of shrieking, diseased and pestilent Falsifiers, frantically scratching at their sores. Dante converses with two shadows sitting back to back, Griffolino d'Arezzo and Capocchio. The Florentine makes jokes about the Sienese.*

The many people and the divers wounds
  These eyes of mine had so inebriated,
  That they were wishful to stand still and weep;

But said Virgilius: "What dost thou still gaze at?
  Why is thy sight still riveted down there
  Among the mournful, mutilated shades?

Thou hast not done so at the other Bolge;
  Consider, if to count them thou believest,
  That two-and-twenty miles the valley winds,

And now the moon is underneath our feet;
  Henceforth the time allotted us is brief,
  And more is to be seen than what thou seest."

"If thou hadst", I made answer thereupon,
  "Attended to the cause for which I looked,
  Perhaps a longer stay thou wouldst have pardoned."

Meanwhile my Guide departed, and behind him
  I went, already making my reply,
  And superadding: "In that cavern where

I held mine eyes with such attention fixed,
  I think a spirit of my blood laments
  The sin which down below there costs so much."

Then said the Master: "Be no longer broken
  Thy thought from this time forward upon him;
  Attend elsewhere, and there let him remain;

For him I saw below the little bridge,
  Pointing at thee, and threatening with his finger
  Fiercely, and heard him called Geri del Bello.

So wholly at that time wast thou impeded
  By him who formerly held Altaforte,
  Thou didst not look that way; so he departed."

"O my Conductor, his own violent death,
  Which is not yet avenged for him," I said,
  "By any who is sharer in the shame,

Made him disdainful; whence he went away,
  As I imagine, without speaking to me,
  And thereby made me pity him the more."

Thus did we speak as far as the first place
  Upon the crag, which the next valley shows
  Down to the bottom, if there were more light.

When we were now right over the last cloister
  Of Malebolge, so that its lay-brothers
  Could manifest themselves unto our sight,

Divers lamentings pierced me through and through,
  Which with compassion had their arrows barbed,
  Whereat mine ears I covered with my hands.

What pain would be, if from the hospitals
  Of Valdichiana, 'twixt July and September,
  And of Maremma and Sardinia

All the diseases in one moat were gathered,
  Such was it here, and such a stench came from it
  As from putrescent limbs is wont to issue.

We had descended on the furthest bank
  From the long crag, upon the left hand still,
  And then more vivid was my power of sight

Down tow'rds the bottom, where the ministress
  Of the high Lord, Justice infallible,
  Punishes forgers, which she here records.

I do not think a sadder sight to see
  Was in Aegina the whole people sick
  (When was the air so full of pestilence,

The animals, down to the little worm,
  All fell, and afterwards the ancient people,
  According as the poets have affirmed,

Were from the seed of ants restored again)
  Than was it to behold through that dark valley
  The spirits languishing in divers heaps.

This on the belly, that upon the back
  One of the other lay, and others crawling
  Shifted themselves along the dismal road.

We step by step went onward without speech,
  Gazing upon and listening to the sick
  Who had not strength enough to lift their bodies.

I saw two sitting leaned against each other,
  As leans in heating platter against platter,
  From head to foot bespotted o'er with scabs;

And never saw I plied a currycomb
  By stable-boy for whom his master waits,
  Or him who keeps awake unwillingly,

As every one was plying fast the bite
  Of nails upon himself, for the great rage
  Of itching which no other succour had.

And the nails downward with them dragged the scab,
  In fashion as a knife the scales of bream,
  Or any other fish that has them largest.

"O thou, that with thy fingers dost dismail thee,"
  Began my Leader unto one of them,
  "And makest of them pincers now and then,

Tell me if any Latian is with those
  Who are herein; so may thy nails suffice thee
  To all eternity unto this work."

"Latians are we, whom thou so wasted seest,
  Both of us here," one weeping made reply;
  "But who art thou, that questionest about us?"

And said the Guide: "One am I who descends
  Down with this living man from cliff to cliff,
  And I intend to show Hell unto him."

Then broken was their mutual support,
  And trembling each one turned himself to me,
  With others who had heard him by rebound.

Wholly to me did the good Master gather,
  Saying: "Say unto them whate'er thou wishest."
  And I began, since he would have it so:

"So may your memory not steal away
  In the first world from out the minds of men,
  But so may it survive 'neath many suns,

Say to me who ye are, and of what people;
  Let not your foul and loathsome punishment
  Make you afraid to show yourselves to me."

"I of Arezzo was," one made reply,
  "And Albert of Siena had me burned;
  But what I died for does not bring me here.

'Tis true I said to him, speaking in jest,
  That I could rise by flight into the air,
  And he who had conceit, but little wit,

Would have me show to him the art; and only
  Because no Daedalus I made him, made me
  Be burned by one who held him as his son.

But unto the last *Bolgia* of the ten,
  For alchemy, which in the world I practised,
  Minos, who cannot err, has me condemned."

And to the Poet said I: "Now was ever
  So vain a people as the Sienese?
  Not for a certainty the French by far."

Whereat the other leper, who had heard me,
  Replied unto my speech: "Taking out Stricca,
  Who knew the art of moderate expenses,

And Niccolo, who the luxurious use
  Of cloves discovered earliest of all
  Within that garden where such seed takes root;

And taking out the band, among whom squandered
  Caccia d'Ascian his vineyards and vast woods,
  And where his wit the Abbagliato proffered!

But, that thou know who thus doth second thee
  Against the Sienese, make sharp thine eye
  Tow'rds me, so that my face well answer thee,

And thou shalt see I am Capocchio's shade,
  Who metals falsified by alchemy;
  Thou must remember, if I well descry thee,

How I a skilful ape of nature was."

☙CANTO XXX

*This canto conveys the mental and physical corruption of
Fraud in its multiple forms. Two mad Impersonators, Gianni
Schicchi, member of the powerful Florentine Cavalcanti
family, and Myrrha, incestuous daughter of King Cinyras
of Cyprus, dash on to the scene. One bites into Capocchio's
neck and drags him away. An immobile, dehumanized
Counterfeiter, Master Adam, explains how his practice was
positively encouraged by his patrons and points to the feverish
shadows of two Liars, Potiphar's wife and Sinon the Greek.
The latter argues with Master Adam. The pilgrim is once
again chided for his fascination with such lowly creatures.*

'Twas at the time when Juno was enraged,
  For Semele, against the Theban blood,
  As she already more than once had shown,

So reft of reason Athamas became,
  That, seeing his own wife with children twain
  Walking encumbered upon either hand,

He cried: "Spread out the nets, that I may take
  The lioness and her whelps upon the passage;"
  And then extended his unpitying claws,

Seizing the first, who had the name Learchus,
  And whirled him round, and dashed him on a rock;
  And she, with the other burthen, drowned herself –

And at the time when fortune downward hurled
  The Trojan's arrogance, that all things dared,
  So that the king was with his kingdom crushed,

Hecuba sad, disconsolate, and captive,
  When lifeless she beheld Polyxena,
  And of her Polydorus on the shore

Of ocean was the dolorous one aware,
  Out of her senses like a dog she barked,
  So much the anguish had her mind distorted;

But not of Thebes the furies nor the Trojan
  Were ever seen in any one so cruel
  In goading beasts, and much more human members,

As I beheld two shadows pale and naked,
  Who, biting, in the manner ran along
  That a boar does, when from the sty turned loose.

One to Capocchio came, and by the nape
  Seized with its teeth his neck, so that in dragging
  It made his belly grate the solid bottom.

And the Aretine, who trembling had remained,
  Said to me: "That mad sprite is Gianni Schicchi,
  And raving goes thus harrying other people."

"O," said I to him, "so may not the other
  Set teeth on thee, let it not weary thee
  To tell us who it is, ere it dart hence."

And he to me: "That is the ancient ghost
  Of the nefarious Myrrha, who became
  Beyond all rightful love her father's lover.

She came to sin with him after this manner,
  By counterfeiting of another's form;
  As he who goeth yonder undertook,

That he might gain the lady of the herd,
  To counterfeit in himself Buoso Donati,
  Making a will and giving it due form."

And after the two maniacs had passed
  On whom I held mine eye, I turned it back
  To look upon the other evil-born.

I saw one made in fashion of a lute,
  If he had only had the groin cut off
  Just at the point at which a man is forked.

The heavy dropsy, that so disproportions
  The limbs with humours, which it ill concocts,
  That the face corresponds not to the belly,

Compelled him so to hold his lips apart
  As does the hectic, who because of thirst
  One tow'rds the chin, the other upward turns.

"O ye, who without any torment are,
  And why I know not, in the world of woe,"
  He said to us, "behold, and be attentive

Unto the misery of Master Adam;
  I had while living much of what I wished,
  And now, alas, a drop of water crave.

The rivulets, that from the verdant hills
  Of Cassentin descend down into Arno,
  Making their channels to be cold and moist,

Ever before me stand, and not in vain;
  For far more doth their image dry me up
  Than the disease which strips my face of flesh.

The rigid justice that chastises me
  Draweth occasion from the place in which
  I sinned, to put the more my sighs in flight.

There is Romena, where I counterfeited
  The currency imprinted with the Baptist,
  For which I left my body burned above.

But if I here could see the tristful soul
  Of Guido, or Alessandro, or their brother,
  For Branda's fount I would not give the sight.

One is within already, if the raving
  Shades that are going round about speak truth;
  But what avails it me, whose limbs are tied?

If I were only still so light, that in
  A hundred years I could advance one inch,
  I had already started on the way,

Seeking him out among this squalid folk,
  Although the circuit be eleven miles,
  And be not less than half a mile across.

For them am I in such a family;
  They did induce me into coining florins,
  Which had three carats of impurity."

And I to him: "Who are the two poor wretches
  That smoke like unto a wet hand in winter,
  Lying there close upon thy right-hand confines?"

"I found them here," replied he, "when I rained
  Into this chasm, and since they have not turned,
  Nor do I think they will for evermore.

One the false woman is who accused Joseph,
  The other the false Sinon, Greek of Troy;
  From acute fever they send forth such reek."

And one of them, who felt himself annoyed
  At being, peradventure, named so darkly,
  Smote with the fist upon his hardened paunch.

It gave a sound, as if it were a drum;
  And Master Adam smote him in the face,
  With arm that did not seem to be less hard,

Saying to him: "Although be taken from me
  All motion, for my limbs that heavy are,
  I have an arm unfettered for such need."

Whereat he answer made: "When thou didst go
  Unto the fire, thou hadst it not so ready:
  But hadst it so and more when thou wast coining."

The dropsical: "Thou sayest true in that;
  But thou wast not so true a witness there,
  Where thou wast questioned of the truth at Troy."

"If I spake false, thou falsifiedst the coin,"
  Said Sinon; "and for one fault I am here,
  And thou for more than any other demon."

"Remember, perjurer, about the horse,"
  He made reply who had the swollen belly,
  "And rueful be it thee the whole world knows it."

"Rueful to thee the thirst be wherewith cracks
  Thy tongue," the Greek said, "and the putrid water
  That hedges so thy paunch before thine eyes."

Then the false-coiner: "So is gaping wide
  Thy mouth for speaking evil, as 'tis wont;
  Because if I have thirst, and humour stuff me

Thou hast the burning and the head that aches,
  And to lick up the mirror of Narcissus
  Thou wouldst not want words many to invite thee."

In listening to them was I wholly fixed,
  When said the Master to me: "Now just look,
  For little wants it that I quarrel with thee."

When him I heard in anger speak to me,
  I turned me round towards him with such shame
  That still it eddies through my memory.

And as he is who dreams of his own harm,
  Who dreaming wishes it may be a dream,
  So that he craves what is, as if it were not;

Such I became, not having power to speak,
  For to excuse myself I wished, and still
  Excused myself, and did not think I did it.

"Less shame doth wash away a greater fault",
  The Master said, "than this of thine has been;
  Therefore thyself disburden of all sadness,

And make account that I am aye beside thee,
  If e'er it come to pass that fortune bring thee
  Where there are people in a like dispute;

For a base wish it is to wish to hear it."

❧CANTO XXXI

*Dante and Virgil leave the domain of Simple Fraud and
journey from the* Malebolge *into Cocytus, the central lake
of ice, where Complex Fraud is punished. The surrounding
silence is broken by the piercing blast of Nimrod's distant
horn. He and other giants are forever fixed to the pit
of Hell for having violently rebelled against Jove. Only
Antaeus may speak and is unchained. At Virgil's request,
he picks the pair of poets up in his enormous hand and
deposits them below.*

One and the selfsame tongue first wounded me,
  So that it tinged the one cheek and the other,
  And then held out to me the medicine;

Thus do I hear that once Achilles' spear,
  His and his father's, used to be the cause
  First of a sad and then a gracious boon.

We turned our backs upon the wretched valley,
  Upon the bank that girds it round about,
  Going across it without any speech.

There it was less than night, and less than day,
  So that my sight went little in advance;
  But I could hear the blare of a loud horn,

So loud it would have made each thunder faint,
  Which, counter to it following its way,
  Mine eyes directed wholly to one place.

After the dolorous discomfiture
  When Charlemagne the holy emprise lost,
  So terribly Orlando sounded not.

Short while my head turned thitherward I held
  When many lofty towers I seemed to see,
  Whereat I: "Master, say, what town is this?"

And he to me: "Because thou peerest forth
  Athwart the darkness at too great a distance,
  It happens that thou errest in thy fancy.

Well shalt thou see, if thou arrivest there,
  How much the sense deceives itself by distance;
  Therefore a little faster spur thee on."

Then tenderly he took me by the hand,
  And said: "Before we farther have advanced,
  That the reality may seem to thee

Less strange, know that these are not towers, but giants,
  And they are in the well, around the bank,
  From navel downward, one and all of them."

As, when the fog is vanishing away,
  Little by little doth the sight refigure
  Whate'er the mist that crowds the air conceals,

So, piercing through the dense and darksome air,
  More and more near approaching tow'rd the verge,
  My error fled, and fear came over me;

Because as on its circular parapets
  Montereggione crowns itself with towers,
  E'en thus the margin which surrounds the well

With one half of their bodies turreted
  The horrible giants, whom Jove menaces
  E'en now from out the heavens when he thunders.

And I of one already saw the face,
  Shoulders, and breast, and great part of the belly,
  And down along his sides both of the arms.

Certainly Nature, when she left the making
  Of animals like these, did well indeed,
  By taking such executors from Mars;

And if of elephants and whales she doth not
  Repent her, whosoever looketh subtly
  More just and more discreet will hold her for it;

For where the argument of intellect
  Is added unto evil will and power,
  No rampart can the people make against it.

His face appeared to me as long and large
  As is at Rome the pine-cone of Saint Peter's,
  And in proportion were the other bones;

So that the margin, which an apron was
  Down from the middle, showed so much of him
  Above it, that to reach up to his hair

Three Frieslanders in vain had vaunted them;
  For I beheld thirty great palms of him
  Down from the place where man his mantle buckles.

"*Raphael mai amech izabi almi,*"
  Began to clamour the ferocious mouth,
  To which were not befitting sweeter psalms.

And unto him my Guide: "Soul idiotic,
  Keep to thy horn, and vent thyself with that,
  When wrath or other passion touches thee.

Search round thy neck, and thou wilt find the belt
  Which keeps it fastened, O bewildered soul,
  And see it, where it bars thy mighty breast."

Then said to me: "He doth himself accuse;
  This one is Nimrod, by whose evil thought
  One language in the world is not still used.

Here let us leave him and not speak in vain;
  For even such to him is every language
  As his to others, which to none is known."

Therefore a longer journey did we make,
  Turned to the left, and a crossbow-shot oft
  We found another far more fierce and large.

In binding him, who might the master be
  I cannot say; but he had pinioned close
  Behind the right arm, and in front the other,

With chains, that held him so begirt about
  From the neck down, that on the part uncovered
  It wound itself as far as the fifth gyre.

"This proud one wished to make experiment
  Of his own power against the Supreme Jove,"
  My Leader said, "whence he has such a guerdon.

Ephialtes is his name; he showed great prowess.
  What time the giants terrified the gods;
  The arms he wielded never more he moves."

And I to him: "If possible, I should wish
  That of the measureless Briareus
  These eyes of mine might have experience."

Whence he replied: "Thou shalt behold Antaeus
  Close by here, who can speak and is unbound,
  Who at the bottom of all crime shall place us.

Much farther yon is he whom thou wouldst see,
  And he is bound, and fashioned like to this one,
  Save that he seems in aspect more ferocious."

There never was an earthquake of such might
  That it could shake a tower so violently,
  As Ephialtes suddenly shook himself.

Then was I more afraid of death than ever,
  For nothing more was needful than the fear,
  If I had not beheld the manacles.

Then we proceeded farther in advance,
  And to Antaeus came, who, full five ells
  Without the head, forth issued from the cavern.

"O thou, who in the valley fortunate,
  Which Scipio the heir of glory made,
  When Hannibal turned back with all his hosts,

Once brought'st a thousand lions for thy prey,
  And who, hadst thou been at the mighty war
  Among thy brothers, some it seems still think

The sons of Earth the victory would have gained:
  Place us below, nor be disdainful of it,
  There where the cold doth lock Cocytus up.

Make us not go to Tityus nor Typhoeus;
  This one can give of that which here is longed for;
  Therefore stoop down, and do not curl thy lip.

Still in the world can he restore thy fame;
  Because he lives, and still expects long life,
  If to itself Grace call him not untimely."

So said the Master; and in haste the other
  His hands extended and took up my Guide –
  Hands whose great pressure Hercules once felt.

Virgilius, when he felt himself embraced,
  Said unto me: "Draw nigh, that I may take thee;"
  Then of himself and me one bundle made.

As seems the Carisenda, to behold
  Beneath the leaning side, when goes a cloud
  Above it so that opposite it hangs;

Such did Antaeus seem to me, who stood
  Watching to see him stoop, and then it was
  I could have wished to go some other way.

But lightly in the abyss, which swallows up
  Judas with Lucifer, he put us down;
  Nor thus bowed downward made he there delay,

But, as a mast does in a ship, uprose.

❧CANTO XXXII

*As they descend into Cocytus, Virgil and Dante see more
and more Traitors frozen in the vast icy plain. Those who
murdered their kindred lie in Caina, its outer margin. The
Alberti brothers, among others, are trapped in a deadly
embrace. The travellers next enter Antenora, the second
division. Dante kicks the protruding head of Bocca Degli
Abati and furiously pulls his hair so he will utter his name.
A traitor to his country, the Ghibelline appeared to support
the Guelf cause. He angrily names and shames five
companions. Dante glimpses two more heads, one feasting
on the brains of the other.*

If I had rhymes both rough and stridulous,
  As were appropriate to the dismal hole
  Down upon which thrust all the other rocks,

I would press out the juice of my conception
  More fully; but because I have them not,
  Not without fear I bring myself to speak;

For 'tis no enterprise to take in jest,
  To sketch the bottom of all the universe,
  Nor for a tongue that cries Mamma and Babbo.

But may those Ladies help this verse of mine,
  Who helped Amphion in enclosing Thebes,
  That from the fact the word be not diverse.

O rabble ill-begotten above all,
  Who're in the place to speak of which is hard,
  'Twere better ye had here been sheep or goats!

When we were down within the darksome well,
  Beneath the giant's feet, but lower far,
  And I was scanning still the lofty wall,

I heard it said to me: "Look how thou steppest!
  Take heed thou do not trample with thy feet
  The heads of the tired, miserable brothers!"

Whereat I turned me round, and saw before me
  And underfoot a lake, that from the frost
  The semblance had of glass, and not of water.

So thick a veil ne'er made upon its current
  In winter-time Danube in Austria,
  Nor there beneath the frigid sky the Don,

As there was here; so that if Tambernich
  Had fallen upon it, or Pietrapana,
  E'en at the edge 'twould not have given a creak.

And as to croak the frog doth place himself
  With muzzle out of water – when is dreaming
  Of gleaning oftentimes the peasant-girl –

Livid, as far down as where shame appears,
  Were the disconsolate shades within the ice,
  Setting their teeth unto the note of storks.

Each one his countenance held downward bent;
  From mouth the cold, from eyes the doleful heart
  Among them witness of itself procures.

When round about me somewhat I had looked,
  I downward turned me, and saw two so close,
  The hair upon their heads together mingled.

"Ye who so strain your breasts together, tell me,"
  I said, "who are you;" and they bent their necks,
  And when to me their faces they had lifted,

Their eyes, which first were only moist within,
  Gushed o'er the eyelids, and the frost congealed
  The tears between, and locked them up again.

Clamp never bound together wood with wood
  So strongly; whereat they, like two he-goats,
  Butted together, so much wrath o'ercame them.

And one, who had by reason of the cold
  Lost both his ears, still with his visage downward,
  Said: "Why dost thou so mirror thyself in us?

If thou desire to know who these two are,
  The valley whence Bisenzio descends
  Belonged to them and to their father Albert.

They from one body came, and all Caina
  Thou shalt search through, and shalt not find a shade
  More worthy to be fixed in gelatine;

Not he in whom were broken breast and shadow
  At one and the same blow by Arthur's hand;
  Focaccia not; not he who me encumbers

So with his head I see no farther forward,
  And bore the name of Sassol Mascheroni;
  Well knowest thou who he was, if thou art Tuscan.

And that thou put me not to further speech,
  Know that I Camicion de' Pazzi was,
  And wait Carlino to exonerate me."

Then I beheld a thousand faces, made
  Purple with cold; whence o'er me comes a shudder,
  And evermore will come, at frozen ponds.

And while we were advancing tow'rds the middle,
  Where everything of weight unites together,
  And I was shivering in the eternal shade,

Whether 'twere will, or destiny, or chance,
  I know not; but in walking 'mong the heads
  I struck my foot hard in the face of one.

Weeping he growled: "Why dost thou trample me?
  Unless thou comest to increase the vengeance
  of Montaperti, why dost thou molest me?"

And I: "My Master, now wait here for me,
  That I through him may issue from a doubt;
  Then thou mayst hurry me, as thou shalt wish."

The Leader stopped; and to that one I said
  Who was blaspheming vehemently still:
  "Who art thou, that thus reprehendest others?"

"Now who art thou, that goest through Antenora
  Smiting," replied he, "other people's cheeks,
  So that, if thou wert living, 'twere too much?"

"Living I am, and dear to thee it may be,"
  Was my response, "if thou demandest fame,
  That 'mid the other notes thy name I place."

And he to me: "For the reverse I long;
  Take thyself hence, and give me no more trouble;
  For ill thou knowest to flatter in this hollow."

Then by the scalp behind I seized upon him,
  And said: "It must needs be thou name thyself,
  Or not a hair remain upon thee here."

Whence he to me: "Though thou strip off my hair,
  I will not tell thee who I am, nor show thee,
  If on my head a thousand times thou fall."

I had his hair in hand already twisted,
  And more than one shock of it had pulled out,
  He barking, with his eyes held firmly down,

When cried another: "What doth ail thee, Bocca?
  Is't not enough to clatter with thy jaws,
  But thou must bark? What devil touches thee?"

"Now," said I, "I care not to have thee speak,
  Accursed traitor; for unto thy shame
  I will report of thee veracious news."

"Begone," replied he, "and tell what thou wilt,
  But be not silent, if thou issue hence,
  Of him who had just now his tongue so prompt;

He weepeth here the silver of the French;
  'I saw', thus canst thou phrase it, 'him of Duera
  There where the sinners stand out in the cold.'

If thou shouldst questioned be who else was there,
  Thou hast beside thee him of Beccaria,
  Of whom the gorget Florence slit asunder;

Gianni del Soldanier, I think, may be
  Yonder with Ganellon, and Tebaldello
  Who oped Faenza when the people slep."

Already we had gone away from him,
  When I beheld two frozen in one hole,
  So that one head a hood was to the other;

And even as bread through hunger is devoured,
  The uppermost on the other set his teeth,
  There where the brain is to the nape united.

Not in another fashion Tydeus gnawed
  The temples of Menalippus in disdain,
  Than that one did the skull and the other things.

"O thou, who showest by such bestial sign
  Thy hatred against him whom thou art eating,
  Tell me the wherefore," said I, "with this compact,

That if thou rightfully of him complain,
  In knowing who ye are, and his transgression,
  I in the world above repay thee for it,

If that wherewith I speak be not dried up."

☞CANTO XXXIII

The poets witness the gruesome spectacle of the Ghibelline
Count Ugolino della Gherardesca gnawing at the skull
of his former collaborator, Archbishop Ruggieri. He stops
in the middle of his gory repast to tell the story of his
incarceration and murder along with that of his innocent
children. The travellers venture into Ptolomea, the third
division of Lake Cocytus, where dwell those who betrayed
guests and associates. Any tears shed here freeze and lock
the eyes in a fixed stare. Friar Alberigo agrees to talk if
the icy layer is removed. He declares his soul and that of
another to be dead but their bodies to be "alive" on Earth
and possessed by demons. Dante breaks his promise.

His mouth uplifted from his grim repast,
　That sinner, wiping it upon the hair
　Of the same head that he behind had wasted.

Then he began: "Thou wilt that I renew
　The desperate grief, which wrings my heart already
　To think of only, ere I speak of it;

But if my words be seed that may bear fruit
　Of infamy to the traitor whom I gnaw,
　Speaking and weeping shalt thou see together.

I know not who thou art, nor by what mode
　Thou hast come down here; but a Florentine
　Thou seemest to me truly, when I hear thee.

Thou hast to know I was Count Ugolino,
　And this one was Ruggieri the Archbishop;
　Now I will tell thee why I am such a neighbour.

That, by effect of his malicious thoughts,
  Trusting in him I was made prisoner,
  And after put to death, I need not say;

But ne'ertheless what thou canst not have heard,
  That is to say, how cruel was my death,
  Hear shalt thou, and shalt know if he has wronged me.

A narrow perforation in the mew,
  Which bears because of me the title of Famine,
  And in which others still must be locked up,

Had shown me through its opening many moons
  Already, when I dreamed the evil dream
  Which of the future rent for me the veil.

This one appeared to me as lord and master,
  Hunting the wolf and whelps upon the mountain
  For which the Pisans cannot Lucca see.

With sleuth-hounds gaunt, and eager, and well trained,
  Gualandi with Sismondi and Lanfranchi
  He had sent out before him to the front.

After brief course seemed unto me forespent
  The father and the sons, and with sharp tushes
  It seemed to me I saw their flanks ripped open.

When I before the morrow was awake,
  Moaning amid their sleep I heard my sons
  Who with me were, and asking after bread.

Cruel indeed art thou, if yet thou grieve not,
  Thinking of what my heart foreboded me,
  And weep'st thou not, what art thou wont to weep at?

They were awake now, and the hour drew nigh
  At which our food used to be brought to us,
  And through his dream was each one apprehensive;

And I heard locking up the under door
  Of the horrible tower; whereat without a word
  I gazed into the faces of my sons.

I wept not, I within so turned to stone;
  They wept; and darling little Anselm mine
  Said: 'Thou dost gaze so, father, what doth ail thee?'

Still not a tear I shed, nor answer made
  All of that day, nor yet the night thereafter,
  Until another sun rose on the world.

As now a little glimmer made its way
  Into the dolorous prison, and I saw
  Upon four faces my own very aspect,

Both of my hands in agony I bit;
  And, thinking that I did it from desire
  Of eating, on a sudden they uprose,

And said they: 'Father, much less pain 'twill give us
  If thou do eat of us; thyself didst clothe us
  With this poor flesh, and do thou strip it off.'

I calmed me then, not to make them more sad.
  That day we all were silent, and the next.
  Ah! Obdurate Earth, wherefore didst thou not open?

When we had come unto the fourth day, Gaddo
  Threw himself down outstretched before my feet,
  Saying, 'My father, why dost thou not help me?'

And there he died; and, as thou seest me,
  I saw the three fall, one by one, between
  The fifth day and the sixth; whence I betook me,

Already blind, to groping over each,
  And three days called them after they were dead;
  Then hunger did what sorrow could not do."

When he had said this, with his eyes distorted,
  The wretched skull resumed he with his teeth,
  Which, as a dog's, upon the bone were strong.

Ah! Pisa, thou opprobrium of the people
  Of the fair land there where the '*Sì*' doth sound,
  Since slow to punish thee thy neighbours are,

Let the Capraia and Gorgona move,
  And make a hedge across the mouth of Arno
  That every person in thee it may drown!

For if Count Ugolino had the fame
  Of having in thy castles thee betrayed,
  Thou shouldst not on such cross have put his sons.

Guiltless of any crime, thou modern Thebes!
  Their youth made Uguccione and Brigata,
  And the other two my song doth name above!

We passed still farther onward, where the ice
  Another people ruggedly enswathes,
  Not downward turned, but all of them reversed.

Weeping itself there does not let them weep,
  And grief that finds a barrier in the eyes
  Turns itself inward to increase the anguish;

Because the earliest tears a cluster form,
  And, in the manner of a crystal visor,
  Fill all the cup beneath the eyebrow full.

And notwithstanding that, as in a callus,
  Because of cold all sensibility
  Its station had abandoned in my face,

Still it appeared to me I felt some wind;
  Whence I: "My Master, who sets this in motion?
  Is not below here every vapour quenched?"

Whence he to me: "Full soon shalt thou be where
  Thine eye shall answer make to thee of this,
  Seeing the cause which raineth down the blast."

And one of the wretches of the frozen crust
  Cried out to us: "O souls so merciless
  That the last post is given unto you,

Lift from mine eyes the rigid veils, that I
  May vent the sorrow which impregns my heart
  A little, e'er the weeping recongeal."

Whence I to him: "If thou wouldst have me help thee
  Say who thou wast; and if I free thee not,
  May I go to the bottom of the ice."

Then he replied: "I am Friar Alberigo;
  He am I of the fruit of the bad garden,
  Who here a date am getting for my fig."

"O," said I to him, "now art thou, too, dead?"
  And he to me: "How may my body fare
  Up in the world, no knowledge I possess.

Such an advantage has this Ptolomaea,
  That oftentimes the soul descendeth here
  Sooner than Atropos in motion sets it.

And, that thou mayest more willingly remove
  From off my countenance these glassy tears,
  Know that as soon as any soul betrays

As I have done, his body by a demon
  Is taken from him, who thereafter rules it,
  Until his time has wholly been revolved.

Itself down rushes into such a cistern;
  And still perchance above appears the body
  Of yonder shade, that winters here behind me.

This thou shouldst know, if thou hast just come down;
  It is Ser Branca d' Oria, and many years
  Have passed away since he was thus locked up."

"I think," said I to him, "thou dost deceive me;
  For Branca d' Oria is not dead as yet,
  And eats, and drinks, and sleeps, and puts on clothes."

"In moat above," said he, "of Malebranche,
  There where is boiling the tenacious pitch,
  As yet had Michel Zanche not arrived,

When this one left a devil in his stead
  In his own body and one near of kin,
  Who made together with him the betrayal.

But hitherward stretch out thy hand forthwith,
  Open mine eyes;"—and open them I did not,
  And to be rude to him was courtesy.

Ah, Genoese! Ye men at variance
  With every virtue, full of every vice
  Wherefore are ye not scattered from the world?

For with the vilest spirit of Romagna
  I found of you one such, who for his deeds
  In soul already in Cocytus bathes,

And still above in body seems alive!

ᚦCANTO XXXIV

Across the lake can be glimpsed the shape of Lucifer like a
windmill through the distant fog. The impotent creature
stands alone in Judecca, the fourth division, immobile
from the chest down, flapping his wings, each of his three
faces chewing one of humankind's worst sinners – Judas
Iscariot, who betrayed Christ, and Brutus and Cassius,
joint conspirators against Caesar. Virgil carries Dante in
piggyback fashion as they climb down Lucifer's back and
thighs. Having passed through the centre of the Earth, they
struggle back up to a cave where a path will lead them to
the safety of Mount Purgatory.

"*Vexilla Regis prodeunt Inferni*
  Towards us; therefore look in front of thee,"
  My Master said, "if thou discernest him."

As, when there breathes a heavy fog, or when
  Our hemisphere is darkening into night,
  Appears far off a mill the wind is turning,

Methought that such a building then I saw;
  And, for the wind, I drew myself behind
  My Guide, because there was no other shelter.

Now was I, and with fear in verse I put it,
  There where the shades were wholly covered up,
  And glimmered through like unto straws in glass.

Some prone are lying, others stand erect,
  This with the head, and that one with the soles;
  Another, bow-like, face to feet inverts.

When in advance so far we had proceeded,
  That it my Master pleased to show to me
  The creature who once had the beauteous semblance,

He from before me moved and made me stop,
  Saying: "Behold Dis, and behold the place
  Where thou with fortitude must arm thyself."

How frozen I became and powerless then,
  Ask it not, Reader, for I write it not,
  Because all language would be insufficient.

I did not die, and I alive remained not;
  Think for thyself now, hast thou aught of wit,
  What I became, being of both deprived.

The Emperor of the kingdom dolorous
  From his mid-breast forth issued from the ice;
  And better with a giant I compare

Than do the giants with those arms of his;
  Consider now how great must be that whole,
  Which unto such a part conforms itself.

Were he as fair once, as he now is foul,
  And lifted up his brow against his Maker,
  Well may proceed from him all tribulation.

O, what a marvel it appeared to me,
  When I beheld three faces on his head!
  The one in front, and that vermilion was;

Two were the others, that were joined with this
  Above the middle part of either shoulder,
  And they were joined together at the crest;

And the right-hand one seemed 'twixt white and yellow;
  The left was such to look upon as those
  Who come from where the Nile falls valley-ward.

Underneath each came forth two mighty wings,
  Such as befitting were so great a bird;
  Sails of the sea I never saw so large.

No feathers had they, but as of a bat
 Their fashion was; and he was waving them,
 So that three winds proceeded forth therefrom.

Thereby Cocytus wholly was congealed.
 With six eyes did he weep, and down three chins
 Trickled the tear-drops and the bloody drivel.

At every mouth he with his teeth was crunching
 A sinner, in the manner of a brake,
 So that he three of them tormented thus.

To him in front the biting was as naught
 Unto the clawing, for sometimes the spine
 Utterly stripped of all the skin remained.

"That soul up there which has the greatest pain",
 The Master said, "is Judas Iscariot;
 With head inside, he plies his legs without.

Of the two others, who head downward are,
 The one who hangs from the black jowl is Brutus;
 See how he writhes himself, and speaks no word.

And the other, who so stalwart seems, is Cassius.
 But night is reascending, and 'tis time
 That we depart, for we have seen the whole."

As seemed him good, I clasped him round the neck,
 And he the vantage seized of time and place,
 And when the wings were opened wide apart,

He laid fast hold upon the shaggy sides;
 From fell to fell descended downward then
 Between the thick hair and the frozen crust.

When we were come to where the thigh revolves
 Exactly on the thickness of the haunch,
 The Guide, with labour and with hard-drawn breath,

Turned round his head where he had had his legs,
  And grappled to the hair, as one who mounts,
  So that to Hell I thought we were returning.

"Keep fast thy hold, for by such stairs as these",
  The Master said, panting as one fatigued,
  "Must we perforce depart from so much evil."

Then through the opening of a rock he issued,
  And down upon the margin seated me;
  Then tow'rds me he outstretched his wary step.

I lifted up mine eyes and thought to see
  Lucifer in the same way I had left him;
  And I beheld him upward hold his legs.

And if I then became disquieted,
  Let stolid people think who do not see
  What the point is beyond which I had passed.

"Rise up," the Master said, "upon thy feet;
  The way is long, and difficult the road,
  And now the sun to middle-tierce returns."

It was not any palace corridor
  There where we were, but dungeon natural,
  With floor uneven and unease of light.

"Ere from the abyss I tear myself away,
  My Master," said I when I had arisen,
  "To draw me from an error speak a little;

Where is the ice? and how is this one fixed
  Thus upside down? and how in such short time
  From eve to morn has the sun made his transit?"

And he to me: "Thou still imaginest
  Thou art beyond the centre, where I grasped
  The hair of the fell worm, who mines the world.

That side thou wast, so long as I descended;
  When round I turned me, thou didst pass the point
  To which things heavy draw from every side,

And now beneath the hemisphere art come
  Opposite that which overhangs the vast
  Dry-land, and 'neath whose cope was put to death

The Man who without sin was born and lived.
  Thou hast thy feet upon the little sphere
  Which makes the other face of the Judecca.

Here it is morn when it is evening there;
  And he who with his hair a stairway made us
  Still fixed remaineth as he was before.

Upon this side he fell down out of heaven;
  And all the land, that whilom here emerged,
  For fear of him made of the sea a veil,

And came to our hemisphere; and peradventure
  To flee from him, what on this side appears
  Left the place vacant here, and back recoiled."

A place there is below, from Beelzebub
  As far receding as the tomb extends,
  Which not by sight is known, but by the sound

Of a small rivulet, that there descendeth
  Through chasm within the stone, which it has gnawed
  With course that winds about and slightly falls.

The Guide and I into that hidden road
  Now entered, to return to the bright world;
  And without care of having any rest

We mounted up, he first and I the second,
  Till I beheld through a round aperture
  Some of the beauteous things that Heaven doth bear;

Thence we came forth to rebehold the stars.